D1431346

COLONEL T. E. LAWRENCE

The Boys' Life
of
COLONEL LAWRENCE

BY

LOWELL THOMAS

Author of "With Lawrence in Arabia," "Beyond Khyber Pass," etc.

Illustrated

THE CENTURY CO.

New York *London*

PRINTED IN U. S. A.

CONTENTS

ILLUSTRATIONS

MAP

THE BOYS' LIFE OF COLONEL LAWRENCE

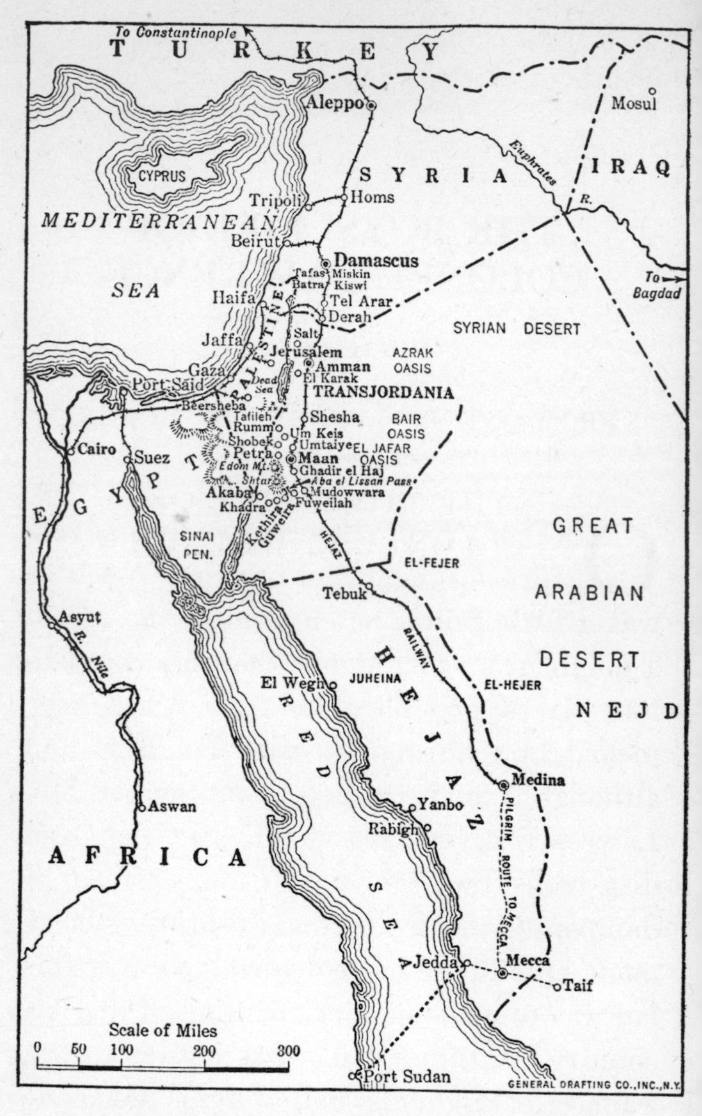

THE ARAB REVOLT AGAINST THE TURKS

THE BOYS' LIFE OF COLONEL LAWRENCE

CHAPTER I

FROM OXFORD STUDENT TO JUNGLE LEADER

ONE of "Ned" Lawrence's first adventures brought him to grief. When he was a little fellow he climbed to the top of a neighbor's roof, higher than his companions dared go. Then he fell. When they picked him up one leg was dangling, and although it finally healed, from then on Ned Lawrence never grew much. But that first disastrous roof-top expedition, instead of dampening his ardor for adventure, merely made him all the more determined. For this lad was to make history for himself and his country. Within a few years he was to win a place in England's hall of fame alongside her most gallant sons, Drake, Clive, Nelson, Raleigh, and Gordon.

The pages of "The Arabian Nights" contain no more picturesque tale than the story of the deeds of this young man who built up an army of wild desert tribesmen mounted on camels and Arabian horses. Ned Lawrence not only freed a country, but he helped win the greatest war in human history, and he even made two of his friends kings of important Oriental countries and placed a third on a sultan's throne.

Ned Lawrence did all this before he was thirty. Our interest in him is increased because he is not a dead hero. But having won fame he now prefers to hide away from the crowds who are curious to see him. At the time these lines are written this young man, who made kings and commanded an army, is somewhere in India serving as a private soldier under an assumed name, helping his countrymen defend the grim Northwest frontier of the Indian Empire against marauding Pathan and Afghan tribes.

I first knew Lawrence, or "Laurens" as his desert warriors called him, in the days when he was leading his Arab army against the Turks, and here is his story.

He came of a once rich family. They were the Lawrences of Galway, that storm-swept county on the West Coast of Ireland which bears the brunt of North Atlantic gales. Although the exact relationship is uncertain, he comes from the same Lawrences that gave Britain at least three other great heroes; one a knight, Sir Robert Lawrence, who went with Richard the Lion-Hearted to Palestine and there played an important part in the memorable siege of the ancient walled city of Acre. The other two were the brothers, Sir John and Sir Henry Lawrence. Sir John was the viceroy of India during one of the brightest and most glorious periods in British history, the period of the Great Mutiny. At this same time Sir Henry was the governor of one of the central provinces of India with Lucknow as his capital. There are few more stirring stories than that of the siege of Lucknow. Sir Henry and a small band of English men and women, and a few loyal Indian soldiers, held out for four long months against more than forty thousand fanatical natives. In that gallant defense of Lucknow Sir Henry Lawrence lost his life.

Ned Lawrence's parents had been rich, but the family fortune was lost before he was born; so his parents had moved from Ireland to Wales, and there, in the county of Carnarvon, a county famous as the birthplace of Lloyd George, he made his appearance in this world. There were four boys in the Lawrence family, of whom he was the third. In order to make it easier for their sons to get an education, Thomas Lawrence and wife moved again, this time to the little town a short way up the Thames from London which is the seat of the most famous of all modern universities.

Here at Oxford young Thomas Edward Lawrence, whose chums called him Ned, received the most of his early education. But not all of it had to do with books and tutors.

One of the branches of the Thames is called the Trill Mill Stream. Its upper waters were supposed to be impassable for any sort of boat, even a canoe. There are many narrow culverts across the Trill Mill Stream, and Ned Lawrence with a companion made the entire journey in a tiny flat skiff. They had lights so that they could see while going through the underground parts, and sometimes it was necessary for them to stretch out flat on their boat. Not far away is the river Cherwell, which the guide-books announced as "nowhere navigable." The two boys challenged this statement and proved it untrue.

From early youth Ned Lawrence not only took keen delight in adventures of this sort, but he also loved to read about the heroes of ancient times, and before leaving Oxford he had made himself familiar with the story of all the wars from ancient Bible times right down to the present day. To him such men as Sennacherib, Nebuchadnezzar, Alexander, Xenophon, Napoleon, Wellington, Washington, and Stonewall Jackson were live persons instead of mere figures in the dead pages of history. He enjoyed reading about them so much that he somehow never forgot the details of their campaigns. But little did he dream that within a few years he would have the opportunity of trying out their schemes of strategy as the leader of an army of his own.

His boyhood companions, and even the members of his own family, hardly knew what to make of him, because he had such irregular and unusual habits. To him these books of history, books that he had been obliged to dig out of libraries because they were not used in school, were more thrilling than fiction. He often read far into the night, and this gave him such a wide store of information and developed his mind so much that his school work was easy.

It takes four years for most boys to finish the regular university work at Oxford, and many have trouble doing it in that. But Ned

Lawrence made it in three. Then he decided to go still farther and get a master of arts degree.

To do this one must write a long essay based on original work and not merely on something copied from the books of other writers. Ned Lawrence thought it would be a splendid idea to set out from England and trace the steps of the old Crusader knights right across Europe to the very walls of Jerusalem, which these knights of old had fought to liberate from the swarthy Saracens. In all history there is no more colorful and romantic story than that of the Crusades. The picturesque followers of the great prophet Mohammed had overrun the entire Near Eastern world. They had even seized the holy places where the Christian religion started. Bethlehem, Jerusalem, Nazareth, and Damascus had fallen into the hands of the Mohammedans. And so great armies of knights set out from nearly every country of Europe to win back the Holy Land. The wars of the Crusades lasted for hundreds of years, and hundreds of thousands of warriors from Europe marched against the Saracens. These crusading knights tore down ancient walled cities and built great new castles of their own between their wars. A special type of architecture appeared during these centuries, and it was Ned Lawrence's dream to write his original thesis for his master's degree on the architecture of the Crusades, after first following in the footsteps of the Crusaders.

His parents were not so enthusiastic about the idea. They feared that if their Ned went off to the Orient he might get the wanderlust and stay away indefinitely. At length they reluctantly agreed to let him have a little money and arranged for him to go with one of the regular tourist parties that visit Palestine and Syria every year. To be exact, they gave him two hundred pounds sterling, about a thousand dollars, for the trip.

The tourist party, made up mostly of nice old ladies and bespectacled gentlemen carrying spy-glasses, kodaks, and medicine-kits, sailed from England for the Mediterranean. The first stop was made at Beirut, a modern city in what was once the land of the Phenicians. Ned Lawrence could hardly wait for the ship to dock. As soon as he got ashore he slipped away from the tourist party, went to the native bazaar, and there exchanged his European clothes for the loose flowing robes of the Arabs. He gave away his shoes and went barefoot, and from then on little was heard of him, except for the short notes that he wrote home. On foot he set out across the country, living with the Syrian villagers and the wandering tribes of shepherds.

In this way he quickly picked up a knowledge of the Arabic language. It was either this or starvation!

From time to time he came upon an ancient ruined city, and there amid the crumbling walls of castles built by Crusader knights he transported himself back in imagination to those adventurous days when the soldiers of the cross waged war with the dashing cavalry of Saladin the Saracen.

When he returned home a year later he still had half his money left. It had cost him but little to live with the poor country peasants and wandering Arabs, and that was what he preferred.

All this happened when he was about twenty years old. His master's thesis was so good, and in it he showed such an intimate knowledge of the Near East, that famous scholars heard about him. Now the British Museum, which sends out many expeditions to study the remains of ancient civilizations, sent for him. They gave him one of their most difficult missions. It was to go alone to a large tropical island near the equator and bring back a report from a remote jungle region regarding some secret digging that the archæologists of another country were carrying on. We shall leave both the name of the island and the nationality of the scientists a mystery, because if the full story were to come out even at this late date it might result in trouble for several governments. When Lawrence arrived at the island he found the tribes engaged in a bitter war. The people on the coast were fighting the more primitive inhabitants of the interior, and Lawrence could not resist the temptation to take part. He joined the jungle tribe and by a bit of strategy helped them win their war. The natives on the coast had gathered together a large fleet of sailing-boats and long war-canoes. They were about to start up the river to invade the heart of their opponents' country. Lawrence got his new friends to lash a number of rafts together and then piled them high with dead-wood and brush. Setting fire to these one night, he and the tribesmen pushed them out into midstream, and in full blaze they floated down to the mouth of the river, where they bumped into the other fleet and sent it up in flames.

CHAPTER II

LAWRENCE ESCAPES FROM THE KURDS

WE can see from his jungle adventure that although Ned Lawrence was a scholarly young man who loved to study history, he also was a person of action and full of the spirit of adventure that later on was to enable him to lead a desert army in a great campaign against the Turks.

After his naval battle he penetrated into the island far enough to find out just what the rival archæologists were doing, and then returned to London to make his report.

A little later he became a member of an expedition that had been sent out from Oxford to uncover the ruins of a buried city in the center of northern Arabia. This region, between the Syrian city of Damascus and the ancient country of Babylonia, is called Mesopotamia.

Thousands of years before the birth of Christ the two great centers of civilization were along the valley of the Nile in Egypt, and a thousand miles farther east in the valleys of the Tigris and Euphrates. The first was the civilization of the Pharaohs, the people who piled up the pyramids and built the marvelous Temple of Karnak. The second was the civilization of ancient Babylon and Nineveh, cities almost as magnificent and mighty as any in our modern world.

But between Egypt and ancient Assyria lived another progressive and highly educated race of whom we still know comparatively little. The scientists of Oxford and London wanted to uncover this civilization of the Hittites. So they sent out an expedition of which Ned Lawrence was a member. Here he worked for several years, helping to explore the ruins of the buried city of Carchemish.

He was a little fellow, weighing hardly more than one hundred pounds, but his muscles were like steel, and his former life among the village and tent dwellers had given him an unusual knowledge of how to get along with these people. Now, this expedition had to depend for its excavators or diggers on the primitive and warlike natives. They were unable to get enough of one nationality, and hence their digging gangs were made up of Arab villagers, giant Kurds from the mountains of Kurdistan, half-Mongolians called Turkomans, whose faces look as though made of butter, mongrel descendants of the ancient Chaldeans who had once ruled over all this region, a few Armenians, and others. But these people are not accustomed to working regular hours. Most of them are as free as the air they breathe. So it is a ticklish business to try to keep them interested in such dull work as shoveling dirt.

At that time Mesopotamia was still a part of the Turkish Empire, but most of these people knew little about law and order as we think of them. They carried their own weapons, and robbery and murder were

LAWRENCE AND THE ROBBER BAND

common. Moreover, each race distrusted and cordially hated the others. So it was almost as hard to keep them from digging into each other with their knives as it was to keep them interested in digging for ancient ruins. Ned Lawrence's work was the supervision of these gangs of half-wild people. He understood them, and they liked him. So he met with unusual success.

All this time, without his knowing it, the unseen hand of Fate was preparing him for the rôle that he was soon to play in the World War. Without all this experience, he never would have been able to unite the Arab desert tribes in their war against the Turks.

While out here in North Arabia, Ned Lawrence had many adventures that give us an idea of the sort of training he received for the most important adventures that were to come. In those days the Germans were doing everything in their power to build up a great colonial empire. They were developing cocoanut plantations on scores of islands in the South Seas. They had conquered many warlike tribes in remote parts of East and Southwest Africa. But what was far more alarming to the British, they had got the consent of the Turks to build an all-German railroad right across Europe from Berlin through the Balkan states to Constantinople and from there across Turkey and on down over the North Arabian Desert to the head of the Persian Gulf. This line was known as the Berlin to Bagdad Railway.

The Germans hoped that it would enable them to get a large share of the commerce from southern Asia and other parts of the Orient which was in the hands of the British. The Germans had already extended their line to within about four hundred miles of Bagdad, and their dream was about to come true. In the meantime the British Government seemed to be asleep. Lawrence, who saw how dangerous this railway would become to the British Empire in Asia, was angry with his countrymen for allowing it to be built. He tried to arouse the British to the danger, but he was so young and so small and seemingly so insignificant that no one took him seriously. From then on he decided simply to amuse himself by annoying the German engineers. So he secretly loaded some long sections of old pipe on the backs of mules and took them up to the top of the mountain overlooking the region where the German engineers were at work on the Berlin to Bagdad Railway. Then he mounted these pieces of pipe on mounds of rock, so that from a distance they looked exactly like cannon. The Germans were completely taken in and sent messengers, both to the Turkish Government and to the kaiser in Berlin, stating that the British were fortifying the hills. Meanwhile Lawrence was laughing up his sleeve.

Of course the Germans were obliged to use local people in constructing the railway embankments and bridges, and they had a great deal of trouble with the workmen. The engineers, instead of trying to learn the names of the Arabs, Kurds, and other natives, simply painted numbers on the backs of their coats. As a result there was no spirit of comradeship or good feeling between the workmen and their superiors such as there was over in the camp where Lawrence and his fellow British archæologists were using the same races in their digging gangs. On several occasions the natives turned on the Germans, and one day news of a threatened riot reached Lawrence, who got over to the German camp just in time to save the Germans from all being killed. As he was already known far and wide in that region, when he got to the scene of the fighting the tribesmen quieted down out of respect for him. This time Lawrence was accompanied by another Englishman, C. Leonard Wooley. News of what they had done to save the Germans reached Constantinople, and both Lawrence and Wooley were decorated with the Turkish Order of the Medjidieh by the sultan, for their bravery and gallantry.

But even after saving their neighbors'

lives, the feeling between the Germans and the Englishmen at the two camps was not friendly. Lawrence had a boy named Ahmed working for him. One day Ahmed happened to pass one of the places where the work was under way on the Berlin to Bagdad Railway. He had worked for the Germans, and when he quit he felt that he still had more money coming to him. This time he saw the foreman under whom he had worked and asked for his money. The head of the German camp came up at this moment, lost his temper, and had Ahmed held and soundly whipped. When Ahmed got away he went to Lawrence in tears and told his story. Lawrence walked over to the German camp, called out the engineer, who was a huge fellow, and told him calmly that if he did not come straight down to the native village and apologize publicly for flogging Ahmed, he would take the engineer there and thrash him before all the villagers. The German laughed. Then he apparently saw something in Lawrence's eye that made him think a second time. Although he was twice as big as the youthful archæologist, he knew Lawrence's reputation. He knew him as the sort of chap who always did exactly what he said. The result was that the engineer made the apology. Of course this was thoroughly enjoyed by all the native men, women, and children who had gathered around. It was a most unusual thing to see a European humiliate himself. So it is not surprising that respect for Lawrence grew rapidly among all the desert peoples in that part of the Near East.

Another time Lawrence prevented a fight between some giant Kurds and German soldiers. The Kurds are a particularly unruly and quick-tempered race. They not only love to quarrel but many of them are bloodthirsty brigands. When Lawrence tried to calm them they at first paid little attention to him. One huge Kurd, a man who looked strong enough to pick Lawrence up and break him in two, pulled back his arm to hurl a rock at a German. Quick as a flash

Lawrence was on him. He caught the Kurd by the wrist, jerked his arm behind his back, and nearly broke it off. The Kurd howled, and his companions were so surprised to see the ease with which a little whipper-snapper handled their biggest man that they soon cooled down and went off.

It was not only Lawrence's surprising strength that appealed to the natives; it was also his perfect coolness. He always seemed to be the complete master of every situation. Some people are born with this gift, but unfortunately not many of us.

Whenever possible he used to put on native costume and go off on a long trip across the desert, passing from one village or Arab encampment to another, living with the people, gaining a still better knowledge of their complicated language and their ways. While on such a trip he was taken ill with a fever, though he continued his journey. He was alone in the desert one evening when he met a wandering Turkoman. Lawrence was on his way from the town of Marash to a village called Birijik. He stopped for a moment to talk with the stranger and asked him to tell him which of two paths he should follow. Then after Lawrence started on, the Turkoman jumped on his back, crushed him to the ground, and began to beat him up. Lawrence was nearing the end of a thousand-mile trip across the desert on foot. The journey had taken much of his strength, and the fever had weakened him still more. So he was no match for the Mongol. The robber sat on Lawrence's stomach and then pulled a revolver from Lawrence's belt. He put it against the side of his victim's head and tried to pull the trigger. Luckily for Lawrence, the Colt had a safety-catch, which was on, and the Turkoman did not know how to work it. Tossing the revolver away, he seized a rock and hammered Lawrence's head until unconsciousness came. Then he stripped him of everything he had. An hour or so later, when Lawrence came to, he struggled on to the village. The inhabitants went with him on horses, rounded up the thief, got Lawrence's possessions back again, and beat the Turkoman within an inch of his life.

On another of these desert journeys Lawrence was captured by a band of Kurd robbers. They took him to their secret refuge, high up on a mountain-top. They put him in a hut and left two of their men to guard him, while the rest of the band went off on another expedition. One afternoon the Kurd sentries were separated, one remaining inside with him and the other sitting outside in the sun. It was a very hot day. The Kurds had had their lunch, and the man on the outside had fallen asleep. The other sentry happened to turn his back, and as he did so Lawrence jumped on his back and overpowered him. He did this without making enough noise to arouse the second man. Then he went out and disposed of the sleeper. The only approach to this rocky mountain-top was up a narrow, winding, precipitous path. Lawrence now had two rifles and plenty of ammunition. Hiding himself at a strategic point, he picked off the rest of the band as they came up that evening.

This tale was told to me by a young British officer in the East, who had seen a great deal of Lawrence in the days before the war. The story had been told to him by natives. I mentioned it to Lawrence several times, and he neither denied nor verified it, but simply laughed in the quiet way that he always had whenever any one mentioned any of his exploits. At any rate this gives us some idea of the reputation the young man was building up for himself before the World War came along.

CHAPTER III

WITH THE SECRET SERVICE IN CAIRO

IN 1914, when the kaiser's armies poured into Belgium, young Lawrence was still working as an archæologist out there in the desert near ancient Babylon. He immediately rushed home, and like many another loyal English youth he offered his services to his country. His thoughts were not of leading armies, nor of making new frontiers, nor of creating kings and princes. He merely tried to join up as a private in "Kitchener's Mob." When the medical examiners looked at him they winked at each other. He was so small that he seemed anything but material for a soldier. Moreover his blue eyes and light hair added to his boyish appearance. He was only about five feet three inches in height, and they told him he was too small. They told him to run along home to his mother and suggested that he wait and volunteer for the next war.

But in the end the laugh was on the medical examiners, instead of Ned Lawrence. What would the members of that board have thought if some one had told them, the day they rejected him, that before the World War came to an end this little fellow would have placed himself at the head of an army, helped drive the Turks from Arabia, Palestine, and Syria, made himself the equivalent of a lieutenant-general, and won the distinction of being one of the outstanding figures in the long and glorious history of his country? I wonder what those examiners think about it all now.

So Lawrence returned to his beloved ruins. But not for long. It soon became evident that the war could not be confined to Belgium and northern France. The battle line quickly stretched a third of the way around the world, from the North Sea all the way across Europe and part way across

Asia to the Persian Gulf. The Germans were joined by the Austrians, Bulgarians, and Turks. The Turks had at one time been the rulers of Egypt. Now it was in the hands of the British, and the Turks hoped to capture the Suez Canal and regain possession of their old empire in Egypt. This made it necessary for the British to defend Egypt and the canal. One of their ways of doing this was to build up a secret corps of spies and special agents who could go among the different races in the Near East and win them over to the British. A general named Sir Gilbert Clayton was in charge of this work, and he called to his headquarters at Cairo all of those unusual Irishmen, Englishmen, Scots, and Welshmen who had been devoting their lives to work of a sort that would qualify them for dealing with native peoples. Among these was young Thomas Edward Lawrence.

At first his job was to take care of one of the offices where maps were kept. Generals used to come into his room to look at the maps and talk over plans. Frequently they would turn to the youthful lieutenant and ask him what he thought of some scheme they had in mind. Nearly always he was able to point out that even though their plan sounded good it would not work for reasons that the generals knew nothing about, simply because the country was strange to them. Lawrence, on the other hand, knew the desert camel-routes, the paths of the sheep-herders, and the half-buried roads made long, long ago by the armies of the Romans, Greeks, and Crusaders. This enabled him to take the plans of other staff-officers and make them workable. Naturally he soon gained something of a reputation, and people in Cairo began to hear of this young man who knew so much about the Near East and its peoples.

But Lieutenant Lawrence, like his friends the desert tribesmen, was an independent fellow. He had never been accustomed to taking orders from other people. For years he had been giving orders. He already was a leader of men. So independent was he that he went right on living his own life in Cairo without paying much attention to the rules of discipline that go with war. Although he was now supposed to be a soldier and an officer of the king, he dressed just about as he liked, polished his boots when he thought about it, which was not often, and appeared on the streets without his Sam Browne belt. So busy was he with his own thoughts that he seldom paid any attention to generals whom he met and even failed to salute them. Of course this caused much comment, for it was an unheard-of thing for a lieutenant to treat his superior officers as though they did not exist, or even as though they were his equals. They overlooked many of his strange ways because they needed his advice. Had it been any one but Ned Lawrence, they would have thrown him into the guard-house.

The first years of the war went by. Lawrence had done such excellent work at headquarters in Cairo that he had already been decorated by several governments. Then in 1915 came the outbreak of the Arab rebellion, the revolt in the desert that was to transform this scholarly young staff-officer into a romantic hero and the leader of a wild Bedouin army.

CHAPTER IV

FIGHTING IN THE HOLY CITY OF MECCA

IF you glance at your map you will notice that the Arabian peninsula appears to be only a small part of the vast continent of Asia. Arabia looks small in comparison with India, China, and Siberia. But it looks small simply because Asia is so enormous. We must compare Arabia with the countries of Europe to get an idea of its real size. It is so much larger than the British Isles that if England, Scotland, Ireland, and Wales were all lumped together they could easily be lost in the Arabian Desert. If you were to place them in Arabia you would still have room for France and Spain, and after that Holland and Belgium could be crowded in somewhere around the edges.

The history of this great peninsula is

thousands of years older than the known history of the British Isles. Four or five thousand years before Columbus discovered America there were great cities in Arabia. Later on we are to go into the desert to visit one of these, a Lost City, with great buildings in a perfect state of preservation. It is a Rip Van Winkle city that has slept for more than a thousand years. We shall visit it with Lawrence's army. In the northern part of this peninsula are countries of which we have all heard a great deal—Palestine, Syria, the land of Moab across the Jordan River, and Mesopotamia. According to the stories handed down from the olden times, the Garden of Eden was in northeastern Arabia. The belief is that it was the region between the Tigris and Euphrates rivers. To-day this is a part of what we call Mesopotamia. Some scholars tell us that Arabia was the first home of our ancestors.

No one knows just how many people there are in this entire peninsula, which was to be the scene of Lawrence's exploits, but there are thought to be between fifteen and twenty millions. The most of these live in the more populous countries around the edge and in the north. The vast central region is a land of emptiness, except for the wandering tribes with their racing camels and high-spirited, thoroughbred Arabian horses. The true Arab is the desert dweller, and they roam about this land of emptiness, living in black tents made of goats' hair. Year in and year out, as the centuries come and go, they wander about from place to place. These nomadic Arabs are usually called Bedouins, to distinguish them from their Arab cousins who live in towns. The nomads do no farming, and they look down upon all who cultivate the soil. Split up into many tribes as a result of ancient quarrels, the Bedouins spend a great deal of time engaged in war among themselves. Most of this fighting is done without much bloodshed. They are great raiders, and an attack is usually over in an hour. The men of one tribe will leap on their camels and swoop down upon another tribe at night. In the confusion they will drive off all the animals and seize any other loot they can lay their hands on. Then the unlucky victims borrow enough camels and horses from some friendly tribe to conduct a raid of their own. They in turn swoop down on a third Bedouin encampment and give them a dose of the same medicine. This raiding goes on year after year. It not only is the chief occupation of the Bedouin, but it is also the national amusement and pastime of Arabia.

The desert is not all sand. In fact most of it consists of barren mountains and rock-strewn plains. The people who live there are compelled to wander about from place to place simply because there is not enough water or vegetation to keep them supplied for many weeks at any one spot. Their worldly possessions are few, and they carry them all on their camels. It is a hard life, and they get so little to eat that fat men are unknown among the nomad tribes. They are lean wiry fellows with thin hawk-like faces.

Although they are of the white race, their skin is so burned by the desert sun that they look almost black.

About thirteen hundred years ago, among these picturesque people, a boy was born who was destined to change the history of the world. He was born in the city of Mecca and for many years herded goats and sheep among the barren hills. Life out there for a herder is a lonely one, and he has plenty of time to think. When this boy was born the people of Arabia worshiped idols and stones. But young Mohammed, for that was his name, did not approve of idolatry. So he made a study of other religions, and in the end he took many points from the Christians, other stories and ideas from the Jews and Persians, and then to these he added ideas of his own. His religion won the approval of his fellow Arabs, and little by little he gained thousands of followers. After his death the leaders who took his place led the lean desert warriors on greater raids than they had ever made before. They had two reasons for fighting now; first to get loot, and second to convert the world to their new religion. So fanatical and dashing were they that within two hundred years Mohammed's followers had built up a vast Arab Empire, extending all the way from Spain and Morocco in the West to India and Central Asia in the East.

But like every other empire it could not go on forever. The lean, warlike men of the desert became soft after they had conquered countries, captured great citics, and amassed wealth. Luxury and vice were not good for them. The turning-point came when one of their great armies met defeat at the hands of the Christian general, Charles Martel, at the battle of Tours, in central France. Had they not been stopped at Tours the Arabs might have overrun the entire world, and even America might be a Mohammedan country to-day.

After that battle, the vast, loosely connected Arabian Empire began to crumble. But for many hundreds of years it still continued to play an important part in the world's history. Then some five hundred years ago another rugged, warlike race swept down into Arabia from the mountains and deserts of central Asia. These people belonged to the tribe of Osman. Their present-day descendants were called the Ottoman Turks. The warriors of the tribe of Osman overran the Near East. Until this time they had had a primitive religion of their own, but they now became Mohammedans. Then, after conquering many of the Arab tribes living on the edge of the Arabian peninsula, the Turks proclaimed their ruler the religious head of all the Mohammedans in the world. The Arabs were now too badly divided to prevent this, and for hundreds of years they were lorded over by the Turks; all, that is, except the wandering desert tribes, who never were conquered.

Of course the Arabs living in the more populous regions along the coast had no love for their masters. They frequently waged small wars with them but in the end were always defeated. In 1914 when Turkey joined forces with Germany and Austria the Arabs saw that their age-old enemies were now involved in a great war against four very powerful nations, the British, the Russians, the French, and the Italians. One of the most prominent Arab families in 1914 decided that this was the ideal time to start a rebellion in the hope of overthrowing the Turks once and for all. The head of this family was an old patriarch named Hussein Ibn Ali. Hussein claimed to be the oldest living descendant of the Prophet Mohammed, the founder of the Mohammedan religion, whose teachings had made the Arabs a great people. Hussein had four grown sons, Ali, Abdullah, Feisal, and Zeid, and the desert tribesmen as well as the town Arabs looked upon them as their leaders. Although the Arabs are a freedom-loving people who regard every man as the equal of every other, they look up to those of their countrymen who are known to be descendants of the Prophet Mohammed's family.

All male members of that family are called sherifs.

The Turks had long been suspicious of Sherif Hussein and his four sons. In fact the sultan of Turkey had kept them in Constantinople under his wary eye for many years, for fear they might start a rebellion. But in 1912 the young Turks themselves revolted against their tyrannical ruler, old Abdul Hamid, the "Red Sultan," and pushed him off his throne. The Arabs helped them, and then Sherif Hussein and his family returned to their old home in the holy Arabian city of Mecca.

Sherif Hussein now sent his boys into the desert to live with the Bedouin tribes. He wanted them to forget their city ways and to grow up into vigorous, daring men. By day they rode racing camels and chased robber bands. By night they slept curled up in the sand, covered over only with their cloaks.

Secretly the sherif and his sons bought rifles and ammunition and brought them across the Red Sea from Egypt and the

Sudan, in sailing-boats and by gun-runners. Then in 1915 they gathered together Arabs whom they knew they could trust and attacked the Turkish garrisons in four cities, Mecca, Jeddah, Taif, and Medina. The first three attacks were successful. The Holy City of Mecca lies in a pocket surrounded by mountains. On top of each mountain was a strong Turkish fort. The commander of one fort foolishly ordered his artillerymen to fire on the holiest spot in the Mohammedan world.

The most famous of all Mohammedan places of worship is the great mosque in the center of the city of Mecca. It consists of an open square, surrounded by a high wall, in the center of which is a small cube-shaped building, called the Kaaba, covered over with a huge black carpet. Embedded in one corner of it is a stone which the Arabs believe to have been dropped from heaven by the angel Gabriel. Hundreds of thousands of Mohammedans come from all parts of the world to say their prayers in the mosque of the Kaaba and to kiss the sacred stone. The Arabs say this rock was once whiter than milk. It is now nearly black and has turned that color because of having been kissed by so many sinful people. The Mohammedans also tell us that the building which houses the holy rock is directly beneath the throne of God in heaven. Pilgrims from different countries hold different beliefs about this sacred place. For instance, if a man from Syria enters the little cube-shaped building he must do so barefoot, and from that time on throughout his entire life he must never go barefoot again. This is because the Syrians think that the pilgrim's feet have touched holy ground and thereafter must never touch any other part of the earth, all of which is looked upon as unholy. The pilgrims kiss the stone and run around the little cube-shaped building seven times, repeating their prayers over and over in loud voices. Ever since the stone was tossed down by Gabriel there is said to have been some one going around it saying his prayers. Occasionally floods sweep down the valley, filling the courtyard of the mosque. When this happens the Arabs keep a relay of swimmers going round and round so that the chain may never be broken.

One of the Turkish commanders was stupid enough to order his men to fire on this mosque. Several shells went through the cube-shaped house and burned great holes in the holy carpet. One struck the sacred rock and killed nine Arabs who were kneeling in prayer. This made the rest of the Arabs so frantic that they climbed over the walls of the fort and massacred all the Turks.

But after this first success the Arab revolt nearly collapsed. The undisciplined hoard led by Sherif Hussein's sons ran out of ammunition. News came that the Turks were sending a strong army down from the north to recapture Mecca and Jeddah. It was at this moment that young Lawrence turned up in Arabia to save the day.

CHAPTER V

LAWRENCE JOINS THE ARABS

OLD Hussein Ibn Ali, Keeper of the Holy Places in Mecca, and his four sons had been in touch with British Army Headquarters in Egypt and the Sudan ever since 1914. Hussein, a man of the purest Arab blood, was the oldest living descendant of Mohammed. So it was only natural that he and his sons had long been plotting to liberate the Arabs from the Turks. In fact, for two years now the British had been supplying rifles and ammunition to the picturesque gun-runners who plied back and forth across the Red Sea, between Africa and the coral-fringed coast of Arabia. The British, of course, were ready to help the Arabs to the extent of selling them weapons to use against the Turks. But supplying rifles and ammunition to gun-runners was not enough. The Arabs needed a great leader. And they found him in a foreigner and a Christian, young Ned Lawrence.

In 1915 Hussein and his followers launched their revolt and captured Mecca, Taif, and Jeddah. The British high officials in Egypt then decided it might be worth while to get into even closer touch with the leaders of this Arab revolt, and so they ordered the Oriental secretary to the high commissioner of Egypt, another young Englishman, named Ronald Storrs, to sail down the Red Sea to Jeddah to investigate and see just what possibility this Arab rebellion might have. Lawrence and Storrs were old friends. They had been at Oxford together, and now saw each other often in Cairo. When Lawrence heard about Storrs's mission he made up his mind to accompany him. So he simply asked for a two weeks' leave of absence. Lawrence's commanding officers were delighted to get rid of him. He was a difficult young man to handle and constantly irritated his chiefs by his failure to pay any attention to military red tape. But instead of going off to the races at Alexandria or to the beach at Port Said as other men did when given a holiday, he sailed down the Red Sea with Storrs. And he has been on that two weeks' leave of absence ever since!

Hussein's second son, the fat and jovial Sherif Abdullah, galloped down from the Forbidden City to welcome Storrs. By now young Lawrence had spent a number of years in the Near East. He knew the ways and habits, the hopes and ambitions, of the town-dwellers, and also of the wandering tribesmen who roamed the unmapped desert. He knew all about the intertribal wars, the bitter family quarrels and blood-feuds that have kept the peoples of Arabia from uniting ever since the collapse of the old Arab Empire hundreds of years ago. He knew that it would be impossible to build up an Arab army of any size without first finding an unusual Arab leader. The desert peoples are impetuous and fanatical, but they will follow a prophet to the ends of the earth.

"If I could just find some Arab leader with the appearance and spiritual air of a prophet about him!" thought Lawrence.

But Sherif Abdullah was altogether too fat and jolly. Lawrence saw at a glance that here was an amiable, cheery companion, but not of the type to arouse the Arabs to heights of frenzy against the Turks and make them forget their blood-feuds.

Old Sherif Hussein had remained in the Holy City and did not come down to meet Storrs. Remaining with him was his eldest son, Ali. This still left two of the sons to be accounted for, Feisal and Zeid. Abdullah told Lawrence and Storrs that these two brothers, with a large force of Arabs, were camped a two-day camel trek to the north-east. The Turks were sending down an army from Medina to retake Mecca and Jeddah. Feisal and Zeid were attempting to hold them back.

Lawrence wanted to see this army, but

there was an unwritten law that none but Mohammedans should ever be allowed beyond the walls of Jeddah. Christians, Jews, and adherents of other religions are not welcomed in this part of Arabia. This country, named the Hedjaz, is known as Holy Arabia, because it includes the two holy cities of Mecca and Medina.

Lawrence told Storrs and Sherif Abdullah that he wished to visit Feisal's army. Both shook their heads. But when Lawrence explained how much easier it might be for the Arabs to get British support if he took his superiors in Cairo an eye-witness report, Abdullah said he would consult his father about it. Although Mecca is not a modern city, and is cut off from the rest of the world, Sherif Hussein had brought Mohammedan engineers over from Egypt to put up a single-line telephone between his palace in Mecca and his governor in the seaport of Jeddah. Abdullah was sure that his father would refuse Lawrence's request. Nevertheless he rang up the old sherif.

Hussein said it could not be done. He simply did not want any Christians to penetrate farther into his country than Jeddah. But before Abdullah hung up, the silver-tongued Storrs asked permission to talk to Hussein. Storrs is famous for his eloquence and speaks many of the languages of the Orient just as fluently as he speaks English. So persuasive was he that he finally got the grand sherif to give a reluctant consent. So Lawrence set forth across the desert by camel. As soon as he saw Feisal he thought to himself, "Here is the ideal man to lead a desert war." He looked totally unlike his jovial brother, Abdullah. His lithe figure, his haggard face and deep-set dreamy eyes, gave him the appearance of both poet and prophet. Feisal liked Lawrence too, and in a short time they became fast friends.

As they sat in Feisal's tent, Lawrence soon saw that his host had just about given up hope. Feisal's dream had been to build up immediately an army large enough to capture the great city of Medina, several hundred miles to the north. But his force was getting weaker instead of stronger. The desert peoples are only accustomed to making flying raids. They know nothing of military discipline and patient waiting. The first enthusiasm of the revolt had died down, and many of the Arabs who had fought during the first days of the rebellion had now unconcernedly ridden off home on their camels and horses. In the meantime the Turks were sending down strong reinforcements from their much larger army in Palestine and Syria. It seemed as though it would only be a matter of a few weeks until they would be able to march down and crush the dwindling Arab forces. Lawrence's sole thought, of course, was to devise some way of using the Arabs to help the Allies win the war against the Turks and thereby help win the World War.

For the straggling undisciplined Arab forces to face the Turks in pitched battle would be very risky. The Turkish commander-in-chief had rushed thousands of trained soldiers down to Medina. He had also sent down many caravans of camels and mules to carry supplies back and forth across the desert, and he had reinforced his Medina garrison with columns of cavalry and more artillery, as well as with armored trains and aëroplanes. But Lawrence now thought out a plan for defeating the Turks by strategy. From this time he became the master-mind of the whole Arab movement. But he carefully made it appear that Sherif Feisal was doing it all. Feisal had faith in his youthful Christian visitor, and with each week his faith grew to such an extent that he and Lawrence worked together as though they were one man. Feisal announced all plans, gave all orders, and appeared before his people as their sole leader in the field. But Lawrence was the strategist who thought out all these plans and, in most cases, saw to it that they were carried out. Frequently he did the most dangerous work himself.

What was his plan? It was to isolate the

Turkish army, and almost, but not quite, surround it at Medina. The Turks, being regular soldiers, accustomed to regular marching and to formations, and to moving like a modern army with all its artillery and supplies, could not get about over the desert nearly so quickly as the Arabs. Feisal's wild followers, on the other hand, could jump on their camels, take nothing but a bag of flour, and ride back and forth across Arabia just as freely as ships can move about at sea.

Before confining the Turks to Medina, Lawrence wanted to drive them out of all the little seaports on the Red Sea that they had fortified. He accomplished this by a series of surprise attacks. The reorganized Turkish army was now advancing across the desert from Medina to Mecca and Jeddah. Lawrence and Feisal left the sherif's youngest son, Zeid, with a small force of Bedouins to check the Turks. They were to harass the oncoming enemy and make the Turks think that they were still confronted by the whole

Arab army. Meanwhile, Lawrence and Feisal struck off north up the coast. At the same time several British war-ships, a part of the Red Sea fleet, headed north also. The first port they wanted to take was a little place called Yenbo. On the way, a number of tribes, the Harb, the Jehuina, and the Billi, galloped up on their horses and camels to join the rebellion. When the Arabs were within a few miles of Yenbo, the Turkish garrison got wind of what was up and fled. So the first step was won by Lawrence without bloodshed.

What a sight it was when those desert warriors rode into the little port! Feisal and Lawrence were at the head of the column dressed in snowy white robes, while behind them were camel-men carrying silk banners, musicians playing weird music, and then thousands of swarthy warriors bouncing along on their handsome racing camels, dressed in all the colors of the rainbow. Lawrence, of course, was the only European among them. Although he had taken off British khaki and put on native costume, he did not pose as a Mohammedan. So it is really a miracle that they did not tear him to pieces. But just as he had indicated several years before in Mesopotamia, he had a quiet way that always won him favor in the eyes of whatever primitive peoples he came in contact with in this part of the world. They naturally trusted him.

Mohammedans usually pray five times a day. When the fighting men of Feisal's army got down on their prayer-rugs and turned their faces toward the Holy City of Mecca, Lawrence would repeat his own Christian prayers.

About two hundred miles north of Yenbo was another tiny seaport, El Wejh. Lawrence and Feisal attacked it from the desert side, while British war-ships bombarded it from the sea. In a few hours it shared the same fate as Yenbo. As the Turks ran off, the Arabs poured in and had the time of their lives looting the barracks and houses. The fighting men of Arabia love looting above everything else, and Lawrence gave them the finest chance that these desert brigands had had for generations.

FEISAL I, KING OF IRAQ

CHAPTER VI

THE TURKISH GENERAL WHO BECAME A BRITISH HERO

WHEN news reached Fakhri Pasha, the Turkish commander, that Yenbo and El Wejh had been taken by an Arab force, the advancing Turkish army was still in mid-desert between Medina and Mecca. The Turks were dumfounded. They had thought the Arabs were all in the hills in front of them. By leaving Emir Zeid and a few snipers in the hills in front of the advancing Turks, and then by quickly shifting the rest of the Arab forces over to the Red Sea coast, Emir Feisal, commander of the Arabs, had deceived the Turks. This was shortly after the youthful Lieutenant Lawrence had unexpectedly joined him. It was Lawrence who had suggested this way of outwitting the Turks.

Now that the seaports of Yenbo and El Wejh had fallen, Fakhri Pasha still had two courses open: to push on south and attempt to recapture Mecca, or to retreat to the high walls and pomegranate and palm groves around Medina. Fakhri made a hurried decision. With the whole desert to the south of him around Mecca and Jeddah full of hostile Arabs, and with the seaports of Rahbegh, Yenbo, and El Wejh to the west of him in the hands of an illusive Arab rebel army, the Turkish general and his men scurried back to Medina just as fast as they could go. They did not like fighting in that hot, waterless, stony desert anyhow.

After the Turkish garrison had abandoned El Wejh, and the advancing Turkish army had hurried back across the desert to Medina, Lawrence took a run up to Cairo to confer with his chiefs at headquarters. An unexpected bit of good luck came to the Arabs now. They were joined by a man who until a short time before had been an important general in the Turkish Army. This man was an Arab from Bagdad, General Jaafer Pasha. He had seen long service with the Turks, had been decorated by them for his skill and bravery, and had led his Ottoman troops against the Allies in some of the hottest fighting during that terrible campaign at Gallipoli when the British and French failed to force their way through the Dardanelles to Constantinople.

Later he had been chosen by the Turkish general staff to cross the Mediterranean in a U-boat and land secretly on the North African coast. Once there he had organized thousands of Sahara Desert Arabs, the fanatical tribesmen known as the Senussi, and led them in a campaign against the British in western Egypt. His Senussi warriors were game fighters, and under the excellent leadership of General Jaafar Pasha they defeated the British cavalry in several pitched battles. But his army finally broke when charged by some of England's finest cavalry. Jaafar himself was taken captive by the British and imprisoned in the great citadel atop the Mokadam Hills that look down on Cairo.

Jaafar Pasha was a brave and resourceful Oriental soldier. One night he made a rope from his blankets, tossed it out of a window, and tried to escape. But the improvised rope broke under his weight, and he fell and broke his leg. While on his cot in the prison hospital, instead of bemoaning his hard luck, he spent his time mastering English. He could already speak many other languages, and ability to speak English came quickly. He was a jolly, cheery, roly-poly city Arab, just the sort that we usually imagine an Oriental sultan to be. The nurses and doctors could not help but like him, and finally the British released him when he gave his promise that he would stay in Cairo and not plot against them or try to escape. About the time that Feisal and Lawrence took El Wejh, Jaafar heard of the revolt in Arabia. He learned that many of his friends and even some of his own relatives were connected with it. Although he had been a general in the Turkish Army, he had served there simply because Arabia and Mesopotamia, like Armenia and Palestine, had long been a part of the Turkish or Ottoman Empire. Being of pure Arab blood, what is known as Bagdadi Arab, he saw the meaning of the Arab movement and one day startled the British by asking permission to leave Egypt and go down to the Hedjaz to fight with Grand Sherif Hussein's rebels. The British saw that jolly Jaafar was in earnest and consented. Within a short time this distinguished pasha was playing an even more important part against the Turks than he had ever played with them. In fact the Arab leaders soon made him commander-in-chief of the better drilled part of the army which was made up of Arab townspeople and villagers formed into an infantry force for the purpose of acting as shock troops. These soldiers were called the Arab Regulars. Whenever it was necessary to storm a trench or a fort or to garrison captured Turkish strongholds, work that the more impetuous

Bedouin camel-men and horsemen from the desert were unsuited to do, these Regulars were used.

So splendidly did Jaafar Pasha fill his new rôle that General Allenby sent for him many months later. When the jovial Jaafar arrived at headquarters in Palestine, Allenby presented him with a much prized British decoration, the famous Cross of the Order of St. Michael and St. George. Allenby not only was a fine soldier but he appreciated a good joke, and he had heard that Jaafar was a witty fellow. So he decided to play a joke on him at the decoration ceremony. He had as the guard of honor the same British cavalry battalion that had captured Jaafar Pasha in North Africa. General Jaafar was delighted. Now he not only had German and Turkish medals won in the World War, but he also had an important British decoration—surely a rare honor!

Well, after Lawrence had done all he could to convince the British officials in Cairo that the Arab revolt was worth helping, because it might be of use in overthrowing the Turks and Germans, he hurried back down the Red Sea to El Wejh.

Here Emir Feisal, the man whom Lawrence had picked as his prophet for the desert war, held impromptu court. Around his tent camped the tribes who had come in to join him. Lawrence now had an unusual opportunity to see how an Arab prince ruled his people. Although most Arabs are hotheaded, Feisal was calm even in the most trying moments. He heard the complaints of every Arab who came to him with a tale of woe, and he decided each case on the spot. It was a picturesque scene here at El Wejh, but little different from the days when that greatest of all Arabs, the Prophet Mohammed, held court here in the desert. Thirteen centuries had gone by. The history of the world had changed. The Crusades of old had passed into ancient history. The center of world power had long since shifted from the shores of the Mediterranean to Central and Northwestern Europe. Columbus had discovered America. The great empires of Spain and Portugal had risen to dizzy heights and then crumbled. Nearly two hundred million people, all of European stock, our forefathers, had established great nations over here in the New World of the Western Hemisphere. The hardy peoples of the British Isles had built up a world empire greater than the empires of Alexander and of Rome. But while all this was happening the Arabian desert and its peoples remained unchanged. In this age of electricity and gas, out there on the coral shore of the Red Sea squatted Emir Feisal writing by the light of a wax taper held above his shoulder by a black slave. Once more an Arab army was starting out on a great raid. Nor was it an army of tanks, aëroplanes, and liquid fire; it was an army mounted on racing camels and fleet Arabian horses just as in the days of Mohammed, thirteen centuries ago.

CHAPTER VII

PLANNING THE CAPTURE OF A TURKISH STRONGHOLD

FEISAL had already won the support of all the desert tribes between Mecca and El Wejh. To the north of him lay the country of the Howeitat, the Beni Atiyeh, and the Ruwalla. He must win them to the cause if he hoped to advance further. The Beni Atiyeh were the first to come in. Far to the north lived Nuri Shaalan, the great emir of the Ruwalla. Fortunately, he happened to be an old friend of Feisal's, so that they were sure of help if the campaign ever reached his part of Arabia. But between El Wejh and the vast desert area occupied by the tribes under Nuri Shaalan dwelt the Howeitat. It was not known at first just what they would do. The uncertainty was increased because this tribe had long been split into two parts by a bitter tribal feud. Before Feisal and Lawrence had completed their plans for the next advance, however, both sections of the Howeitat came to El Wejh. In Feisal's tent they swore allegiance to Hussein and cast their die with the rapidly growing Arab army. The leader of one of the lesser divisions of the Howeitat was old Auda, head sheik of the Abu Tayi, a famous tribe of warriors. Auda himself was looked upon as the greatest fighter in the desert.

Now, the tribes who wandered up and down the vast Arabian peninsula have been at war with each other almost since the beginning of time. These lean men of the desert nurse their grudges. The old law of an eye for an eye and a tooth for a tooth was, and still is, the universal law with them. If Feisal and his new ally and adviser, young Lawrence, were to make any headway, they must get these fierce nomad warriors to forget their tribal hatreds. At any rate they must get them to bury the hatchet until the war with the Turks was over. So during the weeks while the rapidly growing army was camped on the sands and coral plateau at El Wejh much was done toward wiping out these ancient blood-feuds. Feisal proved to be a genius at this. He played no favorites, never lost his temper, and, with the aid of Lawrence and the other Arab leaders, he even brought old enemies face to face and got them to swear that they would fight side by side without attempting to cut each other's throats. For the first time since the days of the old Arab Empire the tribes came together and fought as one people.

While Feisal was holding court and winning over enemy sheiks at El Wejh, Colonel Newcombe, a daring British engineer, and another English officer named Garland, together with a fiery Arab soldier named Malud, of whom we will hear more later, took a mobile raiding column of Bedouins, swept across the desert, and annoyed the Turks north of Medina by a series of lightning raids and by demolishing long stretches of the single-track railway which was the only line of communication that the Turks had between their main army in Syria and their forces at Medina. Newcombe and Garland had been sent out from Egypt after Feisal and Lawrence had already reached El Wejh. Cairo still little dreamed that young Lawrence was going to develop into a great military leader and strategist. Newcombe was a veteran soldier, and they knew what he could do. But, unfortunately, he was captured by the Turks soon after this.

Lawrence had played a prominent part in the coast campaign up to this point, but nothing like the part that he was to play henceforth. As there was no fighting to be done for a few weeks now, and he was of a thoughtful nature, Lawrence spent his days in thinking out various plans of campaign. None of these satisfied him. Then one day the whole situation suddenly cleared up in his mind.

Realizing that the desert war had to be carried on largely by means of the nomad

Bedouins, men who knew nothing of discipline and would have none of it, he came to the conclusion that there was just one thing to do. That was to play a sort of hit-and-run game with the Turks: strike at them at one point, then disappear into the desert, turn up a few hundred miles away and irritate the Turks there, then vanish for a bit and suddenly appear out of the desert haze at another point far away and surprise the enemy again, a game for which the tough old desert warriors were thoroughly trained. It was exactly what they had been doing in their raids on each other for centuries. The Turks, with their masses of troops organized along the lines of modern military rules, knew how to defend themselves, but in a hit-and-run game they could not strike back because they could not move fast enough to catch the Arabs. Wherever the Turks went, their non-fighting supply trains had to go. This would slow them up. But each Arab was an army unto himself. He carried his own food and ammunition, and he depended upon no one. So Lawrence decided that the thing for the Arabs to do was to keep dashing here and there on raids and thus force the Turks to hold a long line. He with a much smaller force of mounted Arabs could appear and disappear and keep the Turks so occupied and worried that they could not possibly be spared from service against the Arabs to go off to Palestine for service in the war going on there against the British.

Lawrence concluded that it would be a mistake to drive the Turks out of Medina. The thing to do was to trick them into holding the city. Let them have their old single-track railway north across the desert to Syria. That would simply lengthen the line that the Turks would have to defend. It would also give the Arabs a glorious chance to run in, whenever they were short of supplies, and capture a Turkish train laden with guns and food intended for the Medina garrison. In fact Lawrence decided that the one thing to do was to compel the Turks to hold Medina until the rest of the war was won. This was clever strategy, and it worked out just as Lawrence planned.

In the meantime, however, the British leaders in Cairo, who were now interesting themselves in the Arab revolt, had worked out a scheme of their own. Their plan was to cut the Turkish railway and then hold the gap against the attacks of the Turks both from the north and south. Little attention was paid to Lawrence. But he worked quietly in the hope that his opportunity would come. He made friends with Sheik Auda Abu Tayi, the tough old warrior who he knew was worth a hundred other Arabs because of his gift for leadership. Auda was a daring fellow ready for anything. Lawrence listened to him patiently, and whenever Auda happened to make a suggestion that fitted in with Lawrence's own scheme he would lead Auda on and on until his pride would prevent him from listening to any other plan.

Perhaps no other European could have accomplished the task which Lawrence now set for himself. If you glance at a map you will notice that the northern end of the Red Sea divides itself into two arms. The sharp point of the Sinai Desert is responsible for this. The arm to the left is the Gulf of Suez, up which passes the commerce of the world. The arm to the right is the little known and seldom visited Gulf of Akaba. Decades go by and not a ship is seen plying the waters of that remote gulf. Thousands of years ago it was one of the busiest stretches of water in the whole world. It was here that the great fleet of King Solomon rode at anchor. It was from the head of this far-off gulf that Solomon's sailors set forth in their galleys to bring back spices and riches from the strange realms of Hindustan and Far Cathay. Most people have never even heard of the Gulf of Akaba. Now Lawrence was to bring it into the limelight again, much as it had been in the days of the Queen of Sheba.

At the very head of the gulf, the Turks had erected strong fortifications and prepared a base from which to launch an attack on Egypt. They had done this during the first year of the World War. They had placed their cannon upon the hills overlooking the tiny Arab town of Akaba so that it would be almost impossible for an Allied force to land a military expedition. The spot was also an ideal place to defend, because if any one tried to approach from the opposite side, from the desert, it could only be done through a narrow mountain gorge. Dotted along this valley were a string of Turkish forts, and the Turks were satisfied that no army coming from the desert could ever capture all of them. So because the base seemed so easy to defend, and because it was located in a place from which Egypt and the Suez Canal could be attacked, Akaba was regarded as one of the most important strategical points in the Near East. Lawrence now made up his mind to try to take it by strategy.

If he could do this it would mean everything to the Arabs, and it would be a tremendous help to the Allied Armies in breaking the power of the Turks. It would enable Lawrence to transform the desert revolt into a far more ambitious thing, an invasion of Palestine and Syria. His plan showed that Lawrence was not lacking in either imagination or vision. But it is one thing to think out such a plan, and it is a totally different thing to carry the plan through. Could an under-sized, youthful student and scientist, a boy of a totally different race and religion, successfully lead a horde of fanatical Mohammedans through such an important campaign as this?

CHAPTER VIII

A DESERT MARCH TO THE LAND OF AUDA ABU TAYI

EARLY in May, 1917, Lawrence set out with a force of Bedouins on his first great raid, a raid that was to prove the turning point of the whole desert campaign. The official leader of the force was to be Sherif Nasir of Medina. But Auda and Lawrence were to be at his side. Many of the Abu Tayi Howeitat came too, as well as groups from other tribes. Feisal and the rest of the host stayed at El Wejh. It is already extremely hot in this part of Arabia by April, so that the men and camels suffered cruelly from the heat. The veteran Auda set the pace for the march. During the heat of the day the caravan rested, and much of the journey was made by night.

Their rapidly growing army, led by the

able Nasir, was still small, and Lawrence knew he could only win by deceiving the Turks. So instead of heading due north along the coast toward Akaba, he got Nasir and Auda to turn the column toward the northeast. Fearing that some of the Arabs might betray him, he told none of them what he really intended to do. They all supposed they were setting out for the vicinity of Medina or some of the less important towns along the railway line between Medina and the Dead Sea. He knew the Turks would soon learn of his movements. Rumors travel swiftly in the desert. So his hope was that he could raid the Turkish railway line north of Medina, make that appear to be his real intention, and then suddenly swing off to the west and swoop down on the great base camp at Akaba. Until it was too late the Turks remained sublimely ignorant of his plan.

Between El Wejh and Akaba lay a stretch of three hundred miles of barren waterless mountains. With him went about one thousand Bedouins mounted on camels, and in all they rode nearly a thousand miles on the raid.

According to European or American standards it was indeed a strange army that Nasir, Auda, and Lawrence led. It carried no artillery, no stoves on wheels with cooks to provide hot meals, and no automobiles filled with important-looking officers in resplendent uniforms. Nor were there any regimental bands. It was an army made up only of a picturesque crowd, all wearing skirts, a thousand desert knights perched on tall camels. Each man was sufficient unto himself. He had no food or water except what was in his own saddle-bags. If you had met them on the march you could hardly have told the leaders from the rest of the warriors. All wore the same sort of robe, and all had their head-cloths pulled down over their eyes and drawn across their faces to protect them from the blazing sun and the driving sand.

Each man carried a little less than fifty

pounds of coarse flour from which to make unleavened bread in the ashes of the camp-fire. This flour was enough to last one man on a journey of more than a thousand miles. As for water, the Arabs had trained themselves much as they trained their camels. They drank deeply at every desert well, and between times would go for days with only a swallow of water now and then. Lawrence ate the same food as they, except for a few bars of chocolate.

Between Syria and the northern part of the Hedjaz the Turks had built their so-called Pilgrims' Railway line. Damascus was the starting point and Medina the terminus. It was known as the Pilgrims' Railway because the Turks had announced that it was constructed to make it easier for Mohammedans to reach the sacred cities of Arabia. Of course, the Turks built it for strategical purposes also, to make it easy for them to rush an army from Syria to the Hedjaz. The most important station just north of Medina on this line was Ma'an. To deceive the Turks regarding his real purpose, Lawrence led his forces toward Ma'an.

Finally the column came to the Turkish railway line, and here Lawrence had his first experience in a destructive game at which he was soon to become expert. Here he planted his first charges of dynamite and blew up his first section of railway. It was old Auda's first experience with dynamite also, and he was wild with delight when he saw the twisted rails and great holes in the embankment after the explosion.

The trek north was a terrible experience for the Arabs as well as for Lawrence. Both men and camels had to go for days without water, and the heat was appalling. At last after two weeks they came to the Sirhan, a great valley where there was grass and a number of water-holes. After coming out of the pitiless desert, to these gaunt men the Sirhan was the next thing to paradise.

They now came to encampments and were in the land of the Howeitat. Of course this meant that for several weeks they must remain and enjoy the hospitality of the nomad families who were Auda's kinsmen.

Old Auda, the head sheik of the Howeitat, was perhaps the most picturesque of all the Arabs with whom Lawrence fought. He was a sort of Bedouin Robin Hood, a slashing, daredevil fighter, and a chieftain whose hospitality was famous to the ends of the desert. Auda had never liked the Turks, and he was overjoyed at the chance to join Emir Feisal in the revolt. He even went so far as to declare personal war against the Turkish Government and issued a proclamation to that effect. He not only addressed his declaration of war to the sultan of Turkey but also to the commander-in-chief of the Turkish armies and to the governor of the district nearest his own borders.

"By the grace of Allah, I, Auda Abu Tayi, warn you to quit Arabia before the end of Ramadan. We Arabs want this country for ourselves. Unless this is done, by the beard of the Prophet I declare you proscribed, outlawed, and fair game for any one to kill.'' Thus read his declaration which he sent by camel courier to the Turks. Old Auda meant exactly what he said, although he obviously hoped that the Turks would not leave, because that would deprive him of the fun of fighting them. When he had arrived at El Wejh, a few days before Lawrence started north toward Akaba, a banquet had been held in honor of the old Tiger and his warriors. It was held at Emir Feisal's tent. While they squatted around the bowl of roasted goat swimming in gravy, Auda happened to remember that he had a set of Turkish false teeth in his mouth. Jumping up he dashed out of the tent, seized a rock, and smashed the teeth to bits. This left him without any with which to chew his food, and he suffered much agony until Lawrence had a British dentist come all the way from Egypt to make a special set of Allied molars for the old brigand.

Every Arab chieftain is a raider. To the nomadic tribes who wander about the desert, raiding is both a business and a pastime.

Auda for many years had been the greatest raider of them all. He and his camel-men would go hundreds of miles just to swoop down on another tribe in the middle of the night. He told me that he had killed some seventy-five men in hand-to-hand combat. But of course that did not include them all. You see he never counted Turks, because he regarded them as women. In one battle or another he had seen nearly all his relatives slain. Although he himself had been wounded more than a score of times, when the Arab revolt broke out he was as full of fight as ever. In one engagement several bullets had passed through his right arm, and it was so stiff that he was unable even to scratch himself without using his camel-stick. Scratching, by the way, is an important part of one's daily routine in the desert, because the Arabs have so little water that they are rarely able to take a bath.

Despite the success of his raids and the loot that he always brought back, he was not a rich man because he scattered his wealth among all his friends. Every wandering Arab was sure of a full meal if he came to Auda's encampment. One of this warrior sheik's most prized possessions was a huge copper kettle so big that twenty-five guests could squat around it and pick dainty morsels from its swimming gravy. So generous is Auda that if a guest happens to mention an object in his presence the old Tiger will give it to him if he happens to have it. One day I was discussing camels with him, and he was amazed to discover that we do not use them in America. He immediately said that he would be glad to give me twenty of his best dromedaries to bring back home with me. Nor was it easy to convince him that it was impossible for me to accept them because of the difficulty of transporting twenty camels half-way around the world.

Auda Abu Tayi was a striking figure, tall, straight, and powerful. Although sixty years of age when he joined Feisal and Lawrence, he was still as active as the younger men who followed him. His hooked nose gave him a rather hawk-like appearance; his brow was low and wide, and his greenish brown eyes slanted outward just a little. On his chin was a sharp pointed beard that waggled much of the time because he talked in cataracts, with a voice that could be heard above the grumbling of a hundred camels. He was a hot-headed old desert cougar and more stubborn than the Abyssinian mules that Emir Feisal used in pulling his light mountain guns over the rocky hills and sand-dunes. Although a genuinely modest Arab, he was like a child in many ways and loved to tell highly colored tales of his raids and other adventures. Best of all he loved to play practical jokes on his relatives and guests. His imagination often ran riot, and he told wild stories about his friends, yarns that he made up as he went along. Many of these were most embarrassing too. For instance, one night around the camp-fire he roared out a story about his cousin, Mohammed Abu Tayi, loud enough so that Mohammed's wives could hear. He described in lurid Arabic how, when he and Mohammed were in El Wejh, his cousin fell in love with a beautiful woman who was as lovely as dawn in the desert. He said that Mohammed had spent every gold coin wrapped in his head-cloth in order to present this beauty with a necklace of gems, a necklace that sparkled like the stars. Auda added many other details, much to the alarm of Mohammed and to the anger of the listening wives.

Old Auda's name means "father of flying." Appropriately enough he did actually love to fly in an aëroplane. Some months later, when Colonel Lawrence had aëroplanes sent down from Egypt, Auda was taken up for his first spin. He kept shouting to the pilot to take him higher, and when he came down he said that he wished he had had a rifle along on the flight, because he could have shot every one on the ground from up there in the plane.

Auda's home, when he was not wandering about the desert living in the usual Bedouin black tent, was in a vast mud palace. The way in which he came to build this structure was curious, and it was not put up until after he had met Colonel Lawrence. The young Englishman told him about the great buildings in London, and Auda decided that he must have one in the desert. In order to get workmen he made a raid on a Turkish post, took fifty prisoners, and put them to work. They built him a house with forty rooms and four towers, but without a roof. No one could solve the problem of getting timbers big enough for such a roof, but finally Auda hit upon an idea. He went on another raid, to the Turkish railway line this time, and there he pulled up thirty telegraph poles and had them dragged across the desert and used as a framework for the roof.

Every Mohammedan (and of course every Arab adheres to that religion) is allowed to have as many as four wives at a time. Most of them have only one because it would be expensive to support any more. But Auda had been married twenty-eight times, and although many sons were born all had been killed in tribal wars with the exception of a little chap, only eleven years old, who rode with his father during the Arabian campaign. The lad's name was also Mohammed, and he was very small for his age, so small in fact that Auda would pick him up by the neck and drop him into one of his saddle-bags. Little Mohammed carried a sawed-off rifle, for all Arab boys learn to shoot almost as soon as they learn to walk.

In one desert blood-feud that had lasted for fifteen years or so, Auda's eldest son, Annad, the pride of his heart, was killed. This was the most tragic episode in the entire life of the old desert warrior. He had hoped to pass the leadership of the tribe on to Annad, and the boy's death made him look upon his own life as a failure.

CHAPTER IX

AUDA AND LAWRENCE WIN A PITCHED BATTLE

DURING the weeks that Lawrence and his followers stayed in the Howeitat country, before starting west toward the Turkish base camp at Akaba, Lawrence often discussed matters with Auda's cousin Mohammed, the same man about whom the story of the necklace had been told. His full name was Mohammed El Dheilan. He too was a great fighter, but he was of a far more thoughtful nature than Auda and was the chief orator of the Howeitat.

Upon leaving the Howeitat country the raiding column headed west toward Akaba. They had expected to water their camels at certain wells on the way, but when they came to them they found them virtually demolished. The Turks had heard of an approaching Arab force and had dynamited the wells, thinking this would prevent the Arabs from advancing any further. But Lawrence, examining the wells, discovered that the damage was only partial. By hard work the Arabs finally managed to repair them and get enough water to carry on. This region of the desert, like nearly all other parts of Arabia, is inhabited by a great many different tribes who have little in common except the same mode of living. But they all love a fight, and so they all joined Lawrence's force. Without consulting the leaders, a party of Arabs swooped down on a Turkish railway-post called Fuweilah and massacred the whole garrison. The news reached the Turkish commander at the important station of Ma'an, just as a fresh Turkish cavalry battalion pulled in over the railway from Syria. The general at Ma'an at once sent the battalion out to break up the Arabs and avenge the Fuweilah massacre. The Turkish cavalry scoured the desert in vain and finally camped at the wells of Aba El Lissan. Arab scouts brought news of this to the raiding army, and the whole Arab force rode through the night and reached the hills around Aba El Lissan at dawn. All that day the Arabs surrounded them and sniped away. The heat was appalling. Although the Arabs suffered, of course the Turks had an even worse time because they could not see their enemy. The Turkish commander found that his position was growing more and more hopeless. In twos and threes his men and horses were dropping. The worst of it all was that he could not even tell how large an Arab force was occupying the hills around him. Lawrence only had a thin line of snipers, for he was trying to occupy all the hills looking down on the Turks, and this meant that he had to scatter his troops. But to make it seem that his force was a big one he kept part of his Arabs racing from one point to another. They would fire volley after volley, then stop, rush to another hilltop, and do the same from there.

At last, however, the Turks were desperate and decided to try to cut their way out. Because of the heat, Lawrence and his men were nearly exhausted. Some of them lay gasping in the sun, crying for water. The old warrior, Auda, found Lawrence resting in the shade of a rock and made some remark about the great fight that his Howeitat followers were putting up. Lawrence sarcastically replied that there was much firing, but most of it wasted ammunition. Auda fumed at this slur and, calling his men around him, ordered them to mount. With a wild cry he led a charge down the slope directly toward the Turkish camp. Lawrence scrambled to his feet and called to the other Arabs to mount their camels. Then they in turn all joined in a second charge, down another slope. Lawrence rode at the head of them, revolver in hand. Accidentally his revolver went off. The bullet struck his camel in the head, and it dropped like a stone, so suddenly that Lawrence was hurled out of the saddle. The rest of the Arabs and their camels charged over him, and he would have been trampled to death had it not been that he fell directly in front of the camel. The charging mass broke in two waves and thundered past him.

The fighting now lasted less than thirty minutes. More than a thousand Turks and Arabs were whirling and shooting and slashing at each other. But the boldness of the charge of Auda and his horsemen, followed by the second charge of the camel-men, took the Turks so much by surprise that they broke ranks and fled. Next morning some three hundred dead Turks lay on the ground around the wells of Abu El Lissan. There had been only a few Arabs killed.

Old Auda Abu Tayi was as much delighted as a boy. Two horses had been killed under him in the fight, his field-glasses were shattered by bullets, and others had gone through his revolver-holster and robes. But he came through without a scratch and roared out that it was the best fight he had had for a year. He said he had not been killed because he wore a tiny Koran around his neck as a good-luck charm.

Lawrence, Sherif Nasir, and a few of the least excited herded the prisoners together. The rest of the Arabs paid no attention to the prisoners. Their only interest was in taking loot. Nothing pleases a desert tribesman so much as the opportunity to grab something valuable after a battle or a raid. They load their camels with loot until the poor beasts can hardly stagger. So after the charge at Abu El Lissan they had the time of their lives packing up Turkish tents, rifles, and supplies. They even stripped the clothes from the dead as well as from the prisoners.

Then they wanted to kill every Turk who still remained alive. They were anxious to avenge the death of one of their best known sheiks, Belgawiya, the head man of Kerak, who had been tortured and killed by the Turks a short time before. The Turks had harnessed him between four mules and then driven the animals in different directions and pulled Belgawiya to pieces. Lawrence, however, insisted upon sparing the prisoners. He had his own plan regarding them. He was eager that the news should be spread far and wide across the desert that the Arabs were lenient to prisoners. By spreading this report he hoped he could entice hundreds of hungry and dissatisfied Turkish soldiers into deserting from their own army and coming over to the Arabs. His plan worked, because within a few days Turks began drifting in from posts throughout the region.

After the battle at the wells of Abu El Lissan, Lawrence was faced with another serious problem. He and his Arabs carried barely enough food to keep themselves alive. Each man had his own little supply in his saddle-bags. Now with hundreds of Turkish prisoners on his hands the food problem was urgent. So Lawrence decided to take Akaba, about forty miles away, as quickly as possible, and he hoped that the Turks would have large stores of food there, enough for a victorious Arab army, as well as for an army of prisoners.

CHAPTER X

THROUGH KING SOLOMON'S MOUNTAINS TO AKABA

BETWEEN the advancing Arab mob and Akaba lay one of the most mountainous stretches of country in all Arabia. Apparently the Turks in Akaba did not consider themselves in any grave danger. They thought it would be impossible for any one to reach them overland because of their forts strung along the Wady Ithm, the mountain gorge twenty miles long down which the Arabs must fight their way. The first of these Turkish forts that Lawrence had to take was at Guweira, facing the curiously flat mud plains at the base of the wonderfully colored sandstone cliffs at Rhumm. But Lawrence's propaganda campaign, the story he had caused to be spread throughout the desert that his wild Arabs were treating prisoners kindly instead of chopping them to pieces, had already reached the Turks at Guweira. They were so far from the main war zone, on the frontiers of Turkey hundreds of miles away, that they seemed to have lost heart. As the Arabs approached they ran out, threw down their arms and gave themselves up.

But Lawrence still expected to have to fight for Akaba. There he was, a lone European who had been rejected when he had tried to volunteer as a private in the British Army. And now, thousands of miles from home, cut off from his own people and without even so much as a wireless set, he was leading a horde of Mohammedans toward a strategical point the capture of which might easily change the history of the Near East. But the fortunes of war were with him. The Turks in Akaba were running low on provisions, and there is nothing that takes the heart out of a soldier so quickly as lack of food and the knowledge that he is cut off from any chance of reinforcement.

If you could have been on one of those grim peaks looking down on the narrow valley called the Wady Ithm, you might have laughed at the sight of that advancing mass of desert tribesmen. To begin with, they all wore skirts, they had no discipline, and many were barefoot. Their advance looked more like a straggling force in retreat, because they marched without formation.

The strange parade came to a sudden halt at a place called Khadra. Two thousand years ago Roman legions penetrated to this part of Arabia. In their systematic way they had built wonderful roads just as Romans always did. Little remained of their road down this forbidding valley except an occasional old Roman mile-stone. But here at Khadra the Romans had built a great well, and across the valley a massive stone dam. This made an excellent fortification for the Turks. Behind the wall the soldiers from the hills around Constantinople had massed their artillery. As the Arabs halted here, chattering and panting and wondering what would happen next, since they themselves had no artillery, more Bedouins from surrounding hills drifted in to join them. The thrilling victory at the wells of Abu El Lissan had raised the courage of the desert tribesmen to a high pitch. Lawrence's army was now so large in numbers that sooner or later it was sure to swarm over the walls and take the Turkish artillery in hand-to-hand encounter. The Arabs were talking about the great time they were going to have killing off all the Turks. Lawrence was anxious to prevent this, and fortunately Sherif Nasir agreed with him. Lawrence had convinced Nasir that the campaign, instead of ending with the taking of Akaba, would then enter into a more important stage. He had pictured to Nasir a greater triumph, an invasion of Syria, and finally the capture of the ancient city of Damascus, which all Arabs look upon as an earthly paradise. Nasir, although a little man, had no end of pluck. To prevent a massacre he calmly walked on beyond the massed Arab horde, right down into the middle of the valley. There between his own followers and the line of Turks, at the risk of being picked off by riflemen, he calmly sat down on a rock. His cool act had the desired effect. The Arabs became quiet. Then Lawrence and Nasir sent word to the Turks that if they wanted to die all they had to do was to open fire, but if they prized their lives they could surrender and be transferred to Egypt, where they would probably be far better off as prisoners than they now were at Akaba.

The sun beat down on the great lumps of lava and granite. The heat, the scarcity of food, the utter isolation, and the effect of Lawrence's propaganda won the day, and the Turks gave up without a fight. On July 6 the Arabs swarmed over the wall at Khadra and poured down into Akaba. Firing their guns into the air in a victorious joy-salute, they proclaimed Hussein Ibn Ali ruler of this ancient seaport where the fleets of Solomon and the galleys of the Phenicians once rode at anchor. A few Germans were among the prisoners taken, and they seemed utterly bewildered. One of them came up to Lawrence and asked him where the Arabs had come from and what they were fighting for.

"Who is this King Hussein?" he asked.

"He is the new ruler of Mecca and sovereign of all this country," was the reply.

"Ach Himmel! And what is to become of me? Will I be taken to Mecca?"

"No, to Egypt."

"Is sugar expensive there?"

"No, it is cheap."

His face was wreathed with smiles, and he marched off, evidently pleased that his fighting days in this lonely region were over, and happy to be headed for a place where he could have sugar.

So Lawrence's plan of strategy had worked out exactly as he had hoped. Akaba, the Turkish base-camp, the most important military point on the Red Sea, was now in the hands of the Allies, and an important victory had been won.

For the next few days Lawrence's army and the hundreds of prisoners he had taken were in a precarious position. They were in danger of starving. There were about four thousand mouths to feed. To keep themselves alive, they had to slaughter many valuable camels. Although worn out from the long march up the coast and across waterless desert and barren mountains, Lawrence now decided to try and make his way over the trackless wastes of the Sinai Desert to Egypt in order to have supplies sent around by sea. It was a terrific journey of one hundred and fifty miles. But he rode through without stopping and made it in two days and two nights. Finally he reached the southern end of the Suez Canal and got across to the little town of Port Tewfik. Many weeks had gone by since he had enjoyed the luxury of a bath, and so he went to the ramshackle Sinai Hotel and spent the rest of the afternoon in a bath-tub, with native servants bringing him one cool drink after another.

Lawrence had slipped quietly into Arabia and helped build up an irregular army and lead it to victory, and now he had slipped back into Egypt just as quietly as he had disappeared. The next day he traveled by train up the west bank of the Suez Canal to the town of Ismailia. That same day another person, whose name now occupies an important place in history, came to Ismailia also. When Lawrence stepped out at the railway station he found the platform lined with troops. The air seemed charged with excitement. A British admiral and a distinguished-looking general, whom Lawrence had never seen before, were striding up and down.

"Who is he?" asked Lawrence.

"Why, haven't you heard? That's Allenby. He has just come out to take over the command of the forces in Egypt, and Sir Archibald Murray has been sent home to London."

Lawrence was delighted. He had heard of Allenby, and from his appearance he judged him to be a man of action, a man who might put new life into the war in the East.

Lawrence was still wearing his Arab head-cloth and flowing robes. He was barefoot, and his face was burned by the desert sun. The admiral talking to Allenby was Sir Rosslyn Wemyss. Lawrence reported to him what had happened in Arabia and told him of the plight of his victorious Arabs and their prisoners. Wemyss at once agreed to rush one of his war-ships down the Gulf of Suez and up the gulf to Akaba with an emergency cargo of food and ammunition. Allenby heard a little of this and sent for Lawrence. He seemed immensely pleased over what had happened, because he had already studied the military positions in the new zone where he was to launch a vigorous campaign against the Turks.

Admiral Wemyss more than made good his promise. He went so far as to move his own staff ashore and sent his great flag-ship around to Akaba. He even agreed to let Lawrence have some of the machine-guns from his ship, as well as several big cannon.

Headquarters in Cairo now began to take notice of the Arabs. The British staff-officers saw that Lawrence was a genius and that, if given unlimited backing, he might be able to accomplish much more in the desert. Next to the original Arab success, when the Turks were driven out of Mecca, the taking of Akaba was the most important thing that had happened in Arabia. Lawrence, however, insisted on giving all the credit to the principal Arab sheiks, especially Sherif Nasir and the old Tiger, Auda Abu Tayi, who had led the gallant charge at Abu El Lissan. Of course this endeared Lawrence to the Arab leaders. The idea of getting all the credit themselves pleased them greatly and made it easier and easier for Lawrence to get them to carry out his plans.

With the fall of Akaba, virtually all the Hedjaz, or Holy Arabia, was freed from the Turkish yoke. The Turks now held nothing in Arabia but the great city of Medina and the single-line railway which connected it with the main Turkish army to the north. Lawrence wanted them to keep this. He could easily have surrounded Medina and cut it off, but he was too shrewd to do anything of the sort, as we shall see.

CHAPTER XI

THE WHITE KING OF THE ARABS

YOUNG LAWRENCE and his Arabs had just captured Akaba, the ancient seaport of King Solomon, when I got the chance to go to Arabia. Accompanied by a staff of motion-picture cameramen and several other assistants, I had been with the Allied armies on the Western Front and in Italy for about a year. Harry Chase, a cameraman who had already spent some ten years in photographing life in far countries, was my chief assistant. And now we were to have the greatest adventure of our lives, the opportunity of going down to Arabia to stay a while with Lawrence and his desert warriors.

In the fall of 1917 we were on the Italian front. One evening we returned to Venice after a short cruise with the Italian fleet. A naval motor-launch brought us up the Grand Canal, where we disembarked on those famous steps in front of the Doge's Palace. The city was about deserted, and except for a few Italian soldiers and sailors and swarms of pigeons, St. Mark's Square was deserted. To protect the beautiful front of St. Mark's Cathedral the Italians had piled up tiers of sand-bags. On one of these we saw an official poster, a news bulletin to give those remaining in Venice the latest information about the war. We stopped to read it, and there I saw a paragraph stating that a man named Sir Edmund Allenby had recently arrived in Egypt to take command of the British and Allied forces facing the Turks to the east of the Suez Canal in the Sinai Desert.

I happened to know considerable about Allenby and his brilliant record as a cavalry leader in the Boer War, and more recently on the Western Front in France. I knew that he was regarded as a born soldier, a giant in stature, and greatly admired by all soldiers because of his enthusiasm and his ability to lead men. I remarked to Mr. Chase that, if Allenby had been sent out to the East, I believed there would be plenty of action on that front in a short time, and that the world would probably wake up within a few months to discover that the dream of all Western peoples for many centuries had come true and the Holy Land had been taken from the Turks. It seemed to me that this would probably be the most romantic and by far the most picturesque part of the whole World War. So we immediately got in touch with the British military and diplomatic offices in London and obtained permission to cross the Mediterranean to Palestine in order to join Allenby's army.

It was shortly after the first advance made by Allenby that I met Lawrence. Allenby's cavalry, infantry, artillery, camel corps, aëroplanes, and armored cars had fooled the Turks by attacking them at Beersheba when the German commander of the Turkish army had expected the blow would come at Gaza. Beersheba is near the edge of the Sinai Desert, just over the boundary in southwestern Palestine. Gaza is the old Philistine seaport over on the Mediterranean coast some miles west. Before Allenby arrived, the Turks and Germans had defeated the British army twice in pitched battles at Gaza. Now Allenby, by strategy, swung out around the desert and enveloped the Turks at Beersheba, and before they could recover from their surprise, he had sent another wing of his army against them at Gaza. The victory was so overwhelming that the Turks fled north across the plains of Philistia. Allenby's cavalry was hot in pursuit. It won several sweeping victories and finally took all of southern Palestine almost up to the walls of Jerusalem and the Judean hills. Then Allenby encircled the Holy City, sent his infantry against the supposedly impregnable rock trenches of the Turks, and captured Jerusalem. At this time Lawrence and his Arabs were harassing and annoying the Turks by a series of raids east of the Dead Sea.

After Allenby had taken Jerusalem, he sent for Lawrence. British aëroplanes flew over the Dead Sea, dropping messages at the Bedouin encampments, telling the Arab sheiks to let Lawrence know that Allenby wanted to see him. Chase and I happened to be in Jerusalem at this time, but we knew very little about Lawrence. In fact no one seemed to know much about him. His raiding and work of building up an Arab army was being kept as much a secret as possible. You see the old Turkish Empire was made up of many nationalities; millions of its subjects were wandering Arabs who lived in the mountains and deserts, as well as millions of other Arab peoples who lived in cities like Bagdad, Damascus, Mosul, Aleppo, and so on.

In building up their army, the Turks did not call for volunteers; they simply took all the able-bodied men, including Arabs and other nationalities, and forced them into the Turkish army. British headquarters in Cairo and Palestine hoped that thousands of these people of Arab blood who were compelled to fight with the Turks would now desert whenever they got a chance and come down to Arabia to rally around the standard of Grand Sherif Hussein and his four sons, Ali, Abdullah, Feisal, and Zeid. The British authorities, including Colonel Lawrence, with Allenby and his advisers, thought the Arabs in the Turkish army would be more likely to desert if they believed the Arab revolution to be an affair started by Arabs themselves and not merely something brought about by the Allies. It was for this reason that they wanted to keep Colonel Lawrence's part in the Arabian war as much of a secret as possible. As a matter of fact this policy did not deceive the Turks and Germans very long; their spies soon told them all about the brilliant young Englishman (of Irish stock) who was the moving spirit of everything that was happening in Arabia. It did, however, have the effect of

COLONEL LAWRENCE AND THE AUTHOR

preventing the rest of the world from hearing about Lawrence and his deeds. This is why almost no one in the British Empire or America had heard of Lawrence until Mr. Chase and I came back with our pictures and story.

When Lawrence came in from the desert to meet Allenby in Jerusalem, I happened to be walking along one of those narrow winding streets of the Holy City. Crowds of Jews with their funny corkscrew curls, Armenians, bearded Greek priests in black gowns and tall stovepipe hats, Russians, Arabs, and peoples of a dozen different nationalities were jostling one another. Suddenly the swarm of people in the bazaar parted to let a group of Arabs go through. One of these was a little man dressed in more beautiful robes than the others. In the desert all true Bedouins have beards, and a youth is not supposed to be full-grown until he has one; but this man was clean-shaven. As his head-dress, or *kuffeih,* blew back, I saw he was fair-haired. He passed within a foot of me, and I noticed also that he was blue-eyed and had a light complexion despite the coat of tan; whereas in Arabia there are no fair-haired people and the Bedouins have either black or brown eyes. Although of the white race, they are swarthy, and some of them are nearly as black as the inhabitants of Africa; because they and all their ancestors had been burned by the relentless Arabian sun. This blond Arab also was wearing a curved gold sword which marked him as some one of importance. I had heard just enough rumor about a mysterious young man, who was performing great feats away out in the little known desert country to the south and east of the Dead Sea, to suspect that this might be he.

The military governor of Jerusalem at this time was the same Ronald Storrs, now General Storrs, who had made the trip to Arabia some months before when Lawrence went down there on his leave of absence. I knew nothing of Storrs's trip to Jeddah, but I had met him often enough in Jerusalem and heard enough tales about his ability to speak many of the Eastern languages, and I suspected he might be able to tell me who this young man in Arab clothes was. Just beyond the famous Damascus Gate was the governor's "palace," a building that had been used until recently by the German and Turkish generals as their headquarters. So I called on Governor Storrs and asked him if he could tell me who the interesting little man was who had passed me in the bazaar. He smiled, pulled away a curtain, opened the door into an adjoining room, and there, sitting in a chair, was my Arab. General Storrs introduced him with words that have since been used throughout the world in describing the man I now met:

"I want you to meet Colonel Thomas Lawrence, the Uncrowned King of Arabia."

Lawrence shook hands rather shyly, saying little. I noticed he had been reading a pamphlet on archæology, and I thought that might be the safest subject for conversation. I knew just enough about it and was enough of an enthusiast to ask questions. He talked in a most interesting way about the things I asked, and I soon discovered his knowledge of the old civilizations and ruined cities of the Near East was perhaps greater than that of any man I had ever met. The few attempts that I made to question him, about his Arab army and his adventures in the desert, got me nowhere. I saw he was modest about his own achievements, and so I stuck to archæology. My newspaper training told me that here was a remarkable man, and here, if I could only get it, might be a true story as amazing as any of the tales in "The Arabian Nights." I did not know how I was going to go about it, but I was quite sure that sooner or later I should have the story.

As I learned that Lawrence was only going to be in Palestine for about two more days before returning to Arabia, with my interest in archæology for an excuse, I spent as much time with him as possible. I told him that I would like very much to go back to Arabia with him, particularly in order to visit a wonderful "Lost City" in the desert that I had heard a great deal about, and which it had been my dream for years to see. He said he believed it would be impossible for me to get to Arabia, and that he was afraid Allenby and also the officials at headquarters at Cairo would not be willing.

Then Lawrence disappeared into the blue again, and for several days I made no headway with my hazy plan of getting to Arabia. About this time his Royal Highness the Duke of Connaught, brother of the late King Edward and uncle of King George, arrived in Palestine as the representative of the king. He came out to present the king's thanks and congratulations to Allenby and his army for their magnificent work in freeing southern Palestine and in liberating Jerusalem, Bethlehem, and other sacred places from the Turkish yoke. The duke also brought many medals along with him and presented them on behalf of the king. Not only were the generals and other high officers decorated but hundreds of Australian,

New Zealander, Indian, Egyptian, English, Scottish, Welsh, Irish, French, and other private soldiers were awarded decorations for their valor. Allenby received the Grand Cross of the Order of the Knights of St. John of Jerusalem.

The duke wanted to decorate Lawrence too, but Lawrence heard of this and ran away. Before the duke returned to Egypt on his way home, the great commander-in-chief, Sir Edmund, now Field-Marshal Viscount Allenby, invited me to lunch with him and the Duke of Connaught. This took place at Ramleh, where Richard the Lion-Hearted and his crusader knights had camped when they were fighting to drive the Saracens from the Holy Land long centuries before. It seemed to me that this luncheon was an excellent opportunity to broach to Allenby the subject of Lawrence and the fighting in Arabia. I thought perhaps he might tell me more about it while sitting at a luncheon table than if I brought it up in his office. So I asked him point-blank if he would mind telling me just who Lawrence was, what he had done, and why the Arab revolution was being kept so much a secret. Allenby then gave me the reasons which I have already given: how he wanted the Arabs fighting in the Turkish army to think the revolt they had started at Mecca was purely an Arab affair. But he said the fighting in Arabia had been so successful and Lawrence and his colleagues had already accomplished so much that it was no longer necessary to keep it a secret. Then to my delight he added that if I wanted to go to Arabia he would arrange it. Of course I jumped at the offer, and within a few days Chase and I had packed up our bedding rolls and his photographic paraphernalia and were on our way back across the Sinai Desert, bound for the Suez Canal, the Red Sea, and the romantic land of "The Arabian Nights."

CHAPTER XII

A NIGHT RIDE THROUGH A DESERT SAND-STORM

IN Palestine we were told to stop at headquarters in Cairo on our way through Egypt. There wc should be told of the best way of getting down to Arabia. Although General Allenby himself always stayed with his army up near the front in the Holy Land, he had a secondary headquarters in Cairo, at the Savoy Hotel. Here hundreds of smartly dressed officers, "brass hats" as they were called, handled the vast amount of detail and red tape without which no modern war can be carried on. At the Savoy, where American tourists formerly stayed, were scores of rooms filled with filing-cabinets and chests of drawers. In these were kept the records of every soldier fighting in Palestine, and of every horse, every camel, every auto, every armored tank, and every can of "bully beef" sent over from Chicago.

Here also was an office called the Arab Bureau where a number of staff-officers kept a record of all the supplies that were sent down to Lawrence and his Bedouin warriors in the Arabian Desert. Other wise men in the office acted as intermediate advisers between the Arabs and the British War Office in London, where sat the High Moguls who decided on which battle-fronts the next drives should be launched against the enemy. The conduct of any modern campaign, even a primitive raid-and-run war such as Lawrence was waging in the desert, involved detail work which the fighting men in the field had no time to bother with.

The officials at the Arab Bureau lifted their eyebrows a bit when Chase and I came down from Jerusalem. They seemed to be as much surprised as we had been. That Allenby had given his consent to our joining Lawrence seemed impossible.

They told us there were two ways of getting to the lonely Gulf of Akaba where Lawrence was then encamped: one was to wait a few weeks, or maybe a month, until the next cargo-boat was sent direct from the southern end of the Suez Canal to Akaba; and the other was to journey fourteen hundred miles up the Nile almost into the heart of Africa to the city of Khartum in the Sudan. From Khartum we could cross the Nubian Desert to the African seaport of Port Sudan, from which we might get a chance to sail over the narrow Red Sea on a tramp steamer of some sort or on a primitive Arab sailing dhow. This route sounded the most romantic, and we decided to go that way.

One of the officers at the Arab Bureau jokingly remarked that we were headed for a region as far off the beaten track as Timbuktu. Said he:

"You will find no hotel flunkeys at the

pier to meet you and take your bags. In fact you won't even find a pier. And when you get ashore you will discover there are no hotels. Even the native huts will be so full of fleas that you will be glad to sleep out under a date-palm with a block of coral for your pillow."

Long centuries ago the Gulf of Akaba, the eastern arm of the upper Red Sea, teemed with activity. That was three thousand years ago, in the days when King Solomon's fleets plied up and down the gulf, propelled by galley-slaves leaning on their long oars. For nearly a thousand years now it had seldom been visited, except once in a long time when a tramp wind-jammer on its way back to Europe from Borneo with a load of cocoanuts lost its way in a gale.

"Nor will you find much to eat down there in that dry Arabian Desert," said a general. "Even the bread will be of the unleavened native variety, baked in the ashes of an Arab camp-fire. Of course you will have dates, if they are ripe. As a special delicacy you may be fed on fried grasshoppers."

We took the officer's hint and bought a crate of canned fruit, many bars of milk chocolate, and other luxuries in the Cairo bazaar. We stuffed the cracks of our camera-cases with cigarettes, which we were told would come in handy for presents to the Bedouins. But the day we landed in Arabia the thermometer must have stood above the melting-point of chocolate, for when we opened the kit-bag in which we carried most of our odds and ends we found a new Arabian variety of fudge. Such a hodge-podge of bullets, matches, cigarettes, pencils, note-books, and chocolate you never saw!

One scorching hot Egyptian night we piled our paraphernalia aboard the Nile train in Cairo and started toward the Sudan. It was so hot that we decided to stop for a day at the city of Luxor. In pre-war days thousands of tourists had visited Luxor every year to see the wonderful sights of the Valley of the Kings, and to stand in awe beneath the vast columns of the world-renowned Temple of Karnak, the most majestic building ever erected by the hand of man.

During wartime all tourist travel was cut off, and when Chase and I stepped from the train at Luxor we were welcomed by a mighty shout from a crowd of guides. They nearly pulled our coats from our backs, so eager were they to see who was to have the job of taking us to see the sights. The guides from the Luxor Hotel finally won the battle. They formed a sort of flying wedge and carried what was left of us to their ramshackle carriage, a contraption that the Egyptians call a gharry. As we went careening down the street, between row after row of deserted tourist shops, the rest of the guides came dancing along behind us like a crowd of howling dervishes. Next morning we set out on donkeys for Karnak, with a mournful old graybeard dressed in kimono, turban, and sandals for our companion. Nearly the entire way to the mighty pillars of Hundred-

Gated Thebes he whined out his tale of woe:

"Me guide here thirty-five years, and so help me Allah, the only real tourist in the world is you American. If American see something he want he say, 'How much?' Then no matter what price you reply he say, 'All right, wrap 'er up!' Before the war me no more bother guiding anybody but you American than a white hunter bother to shoot a little bird when he see an elephant."

From Luxor we journeyed up the Nile by river boat and train, and then crossed the desert to Khartum, the gateway to the African jungle. The first night we were here a high government official invited me to dine at his bungalow. It was known as the House of the Hippopotamus Head, because over the outer doorway was a huge hippo skull. Dinner was served in a courtyard beneath the stars. It was a lovely tropical night with a soft desert breeze fanning us. On the table were tall candles, and silent native servants dressed in white filed in with silver platters heaped with all the delicacies of the Sudan.

Suddenly I noticed my host's face turn pale. Turning and looking above the wall of the courtyard I saw the reason. The sky to the east had turned blacker than a moonless night. Reaching up to the height of several thousand feet were great billowy black clouds. It looked as though a range of mountains were rolling toward us. I had heard of this phenomenon before. Our host calmly remarked that a *huboob* was coming, a dreaded North African sand-storm. So the dinner party ended then and there.

The only other guests were an officer and his wife. They rushed for their carriage, without even saying good night, hoping to get back to their children before the storm broke. I had come to the House of the Hippopotamus Head mounted on a donkey. The donkey is still the most popular means of locomotion in Khartum, although the flivver is fast taking his place. Jumping on my diminutive mount, I said a hurried good night to the colonel and started for the Charles Gordon Hotel, half a mile away.

The night breeze had vanished now, and the world was as silent as the inner vault of Tut-ankh-Amen's tomb. The stars overhead and all around twinkled radiantly, but straight ahead to the east was that churning wall of sand. It was rolling toward us with incredible speed. I saw there was no chance of reaching the hotel ahead of it. Soon it had reached the outskirts of Khartum. Now the top of the wall was so high that it was lost from sight. Fine particles of sand began to sting my face. It seemed as though the end of the world were approaching. When the full force of the *huboob* smote us, the sand stung like needles and completely blinded me. I lay over on the neck of the little donkey and left it to him to find the way. After a while he brought me out at the main square in front of the hotel. But even when I got inside I found that the sand was sweeping through crevices in the doors and windows. It was a stifling night; although I have been through cyclones in the Mississippi Valley, cloud-bursts in the Rocky Mountains, blizzards in the Far North, and typhoons and sumatras in the East, never had I encountered such an unearthly thing as this Sudan *huboob*.

Before leaving Khartum and starting across the desert toward the Red Sea, Chase and I visited the most interesting character in this part of Africa. He was known as a holy man. So rich had he become as a result of the gifts of the natives that he even wielded considerable influence among the Europeans. General Allenby needed vast quantities of grain for his cavalry horses in Palestine. But the Sudanese people were reluctant to part with their supplies. The British knew that if they could get this holy man to start the movement by selling his grain, then perhaps his followers would do likewise. The officials in Khartum thought it might please the great man if they sent two American travelers to call upon him.

We journeyed to his home in a magnificent state gharry owned by the British government and all covered with jingling trappings. It was drawn by high-spirited white horses, and the driver was a wild-eyed fuzzy-wuzzy, whose crinkly hair stood out in all directions. Lashing his horses he tore across the desert to the village of Berri. The holy man, Sherif Yusef El Hindi, was standing in front of his palace gate awaiting us. He was a tall, thin-faced, stately Arab with all the poise and dignity of his race. He wore sandals, a beautiful robe of green and white silk, and a bulging green turban. His eyes were like dark hypnotic pools. He led us into his garden and there entertained us by bringing out the longest array of colored drinks that we had ever seen. They were in vessels of many shapes, from cut-glass tumblers to goblets of silver. The custom of the country demanded that we at least sip a bit from each, and we found this not easy. Although the holy man's palace was made of mud, like some that you see in Mexico, inside it was as beautiful as a colored picture in your copy of "The Arabian Nights." To my great amazement I discovered that

Sherif Yusef El Hindi spoke English fluently. What startled me most of all was to find that he knew more about little details of American history than I. His manners were those of an Oriental prince and his voice bell-like. After we had talked to him for a few minutes we were no longer surprised that the people of the Sudan held him in such great respect. He was indeed wise and learned, and a man of charming manners.

The way in which he makes his living is interesting. For instance, when a baby is born in this part of Africa the father comes and throws himself at the feet of the holy man, saying as he does so:

"O noble one, what name must I bestow upon my infant?"

To which Sherif Yusef El Hindi replies: "O child of great faith, arise! Go thy way and return again upon the morrow."

When the proud parent comes back, the sherif says to him: "In a dream last night our Prophet, may his name be praised, appeared and told me that your faith was to be rewarded and that your little girl shall be blessed with the name of his own daughter, Fatima. Five dollars, please!"

CHAPTER XIII

ACROSS THE RED SEA ON A TRAMP STEAMER

FROM Khartum we rolled across the vast desert of the Sudan aboard a pure white train, with double walls like a refrigerator to keep it cool within. Upon reaching the neat-looking little sea-coast town of Port Sudan we were delighted to find that there was a dingy old tramp steamer getting ready to cross the Red Sea to Akaba. It had a number of huge wooden patches on its sides where holes had been made by torpedoes discharged by German submarines when she cruised in the Mediterranean. Now in her last feeble days the battle-scarred old cargo-boat was being used to convey supplies across the Red Sea to Colonel Lawrence and his Arab warriors.

And what a motley cargo and crew we had on the old *Ozarda!* There were 226 Sudanese sheep, 150 horses and mules from far-off America and Australia, sixty-seven donkeys from Abyssinia, ninety-eight soldiers who had deserted from the Turkish army, eighty-two Egyptian peasants who were going across to act as laborers at one of Lawrence's supply camps, thirty-four Highlanders in kilts, and six natty British officers. The ark's crew was made up of an even stranger crowd; there were Hindus, Mohammedans from Java, black Somalis, Berberines, and fuzzy-wuzzies. The skipper of this floating human zoo was a roly-poly, merry-faced Scot who kept us roaring with his jokes. I doubt if old Captain Kidd himself ever had a stranger crowd aboard his pirate ship.

Nearly all of these different national groups did their own cooking in different parts of the ship. So after we had been at sea for a few meals you can imagine what the *Ozarda's* deck looked like—and what it smelled like. One desert warrior aboard our ark came from a waterless part of Africa where water was so precious that it was only used for drinking purposes. He knew nothing about bathing. But there was another man from India who went to the other extreme and had a bath four or five times a day. He took it right out on the deck where every one could watch him and poured it over himself with a cup while the rest of the crowd stood around roaring with laughter. The kilted Scotties nicknamed him Bathing Bert.

The Egyptians who were with us provided their full share of entertainment. These fellows dearly loved to dance. It seemed to be a religious ceremony with them. They would form a great circle out on the forward deck, and while several played on wind instruments and drums the others danced and danced until many fell over in a dead faint from sheer exhaustion. When a man fainted it was regarded as a special honor, for his companions thought that God had smiled on him, and had simply taken his spirit off to heaven for a few minutes!

Naturally sleeping accommodations were somewhat primitive on our prehistoric tramp steamer. Chase and I slept on deck next to the donkeys and mules. The one nearest me looked as though she had come from Missouri, and she seemed to be worrying about things back home, because she kicked nearly all night long and did not sleep well. Neither did we.

Cheeriest of all the British officers was Captain Corble, who before the war had been a banker in London. Corble was also a big-game hunter. He had one bad eye that seemed to be looking straight through you no matter where you stood. He walked all hunched over and with a monocle squeezed in his other eye. He used to tell us stories morning, noon, and night. Whenever we preferred to take a siesta we would dodge the jovial captain by giving cigarettes to the Turkish deserters and getting them to stand around and listen to his tales. Although they knew no English, they were polite enough to laugh when he laughed, and that satisfied him and made it easier for the rest of us. Here was one of his favorite yarns, one that he told over and over again:

"I was out hunting lions in Africa one day, and suddenly a big fellow with a long mane jumped at me from a near-by bush. I ducked my head just in time, and he went right on over me. I thought he would probably come after me again, but nothing happened for many minutes, and so I got down on my knees and crawled through the long grass until I came to an open space. There I saw that same old lion—practising low jumps!"

On our voyage up the Red Sea the sun beat down on the deck of the *Ozarda* and made life almost unbearable. At last we entered the Gulf of Akaba. On our left were the jagged, treeless mountains of Sinai, from a summit of which Moses came down with the tablets of stone. On our right were the equally barren saw-tooth peaks of a mountain range named after King Solomon. One morning when we woke up just after dawn we saw land in front of us as well as on both sides of us, and we knew that we had at last reached the head of the lonely gulf. Along the beach was a fringe of waving palm-trees just as you would imagine there would be. Two enormous flat scows were coming out from the shore. When they came alongside our hatches opened, and all the supplies and animals were picked up by a great crane, lifted over the side of the *Ozarda,* and lowered on to a scow. The Red Sea is supposed to be infested by more sharks than any other body of water in the whole world. And we were ready to believe it too, after what we saw at Akaba. A fractious mule kicked a poor little donkey right off the edge of a scow into the water. The donkey had hardly touched the water before he was seized by sharks and pulled right in two. Then the wolves of the sea disappeared with him under the waves.

We went ashore in one of the long-boats

from the ship, and when we were midway to the beach we heard the sound of firing. There was a regular fusillade of shots, and we were afraid that the Turks might have recaptured Akaba and were giving us a hot reception. But the boat kept right on, and when we pulled up at the beach we found the shore lined with several thousand wild-looking desert tribesmen, all dressed in skirts, with long hair and head-cloths. Each man had a rifle and a revolver or two, which he kept popping off into the air. A British officer who came down to greet us told us not to be alarmed, as this was simply the Arab way of giving us a cordial but noisy welcome. I looked at the weapons that the Arabs were using and it seemed as though almost every type of rifle in the world was represented.

It was indeed a picturesque landing that we made. We had come in on a tramp steamer in company with men of some twenty nationalities. We had landed on a sandy beach lined with Arab warriors. In the background were the tall date-palms.

And looming above these tree-tops were the jagged forlorn peaks of King Solomon's Mountains. Behind the fringe of palms were the huts of the little Arab city of Akaba. We passed to the left of these and followed the shore for about a mile. At one point we came upon a barbed wire stockade, inside of which were vast piles of ammunition boxes and food supplies. This was the supply depot for Lawrence's army. Beyond the barbed wire we came to a cluster of white tents where the British officers lived who were associated with Colonel Lawrence. It would have been an ideal spot but for the insects. Even when the heat was at its worst all we had to do to cool off was to run down and plunge into the cool waters of the gulf.

When we arrived we found that Colonel Lawrence was somewhere off in the blue on one of his mysterious expeditions. But that same afternoon he came riding down the Wady Ithm on his tall white camel.

Life there at Akaba was different from anything we had ever encountered. Instead of sleeping until seven or eight o'clock, as so many people do in more civilized countries, the whole camp was astir at dawn. For an alarm-clock we had a Mohammedan priest, the imam, as he was called. He would climb to the highest sand-dune and wake every one within hearing by singing out the morning call, through his nose, in such penetrating tones that he even aroused the animals. Emir Feisal, the active Arab leader of the army, was camped here at Akaba when we arrived. So important was he that a special call to prayer was always intoned softly at the door of his tent:

"Praise be to Allah who makes day succeed the night!"

A few minutes later one of the emir's black Abyssinian slaves would appear with cups of sweetened coffee. Arabia is a part of the world where slavery has not been abolished. But the Arab is such a lover of freedom that he treats his slaves just as he does any one else. For instance, Emir Feisal would let his Abyssinians help themselves from his bag of gold whenever they happened to need anything. No matter how much they took, he would raise no objection, and as a result they were entirely faithful to him and never thought of imposing on him.

An hour after dawn breakfast would be served in Emir Feisal's tent, where every one squatted around in Bedouin fashion. Instead of patent breakfast foods from Battle Creek, followed by ham and eggs, breakfast in Emir Feisal's tent consisted of richly spiced puffed bread, dishes of small white seeds called durra, dates, and glasses of sweetened tea. From then on until eight o'clock, the emir and Colonel Lawrence would talk over what might happen that day, and sometimes Feisal would dictate to his secretary.

At 8 A. M. the emir, and sometimes Colonel Lawrence too, would hold court in the royal diwan tent. The emir would sit on a great rug of state. All who wished to see him, either to discuss plans of war or to make petty complaints, would sit in a great circle just outside the tent-flap. The emir saw them all in turn, and his patience seemed never to end. He always decided everything on the spot, and no cases were held over as in our Western countries.

There were strange things to be decided upon too. For instance, one day a member of Lawrence's body-guard complained that one of his companions had the evil eye. Said he:

"O Sea of Justice, yonder fellow looked at my camel, and straightway it went lame."

Lawrence solved this knotty problem by putting the man charged with the evil eye on the lame camel and by turning the latter's mount over to the Arab who made the complaint. Decisions were accepted without a murmur.

It is a curious fact that there are no blue-eyed Arabs, and the people of Arabia for some strange reason are terrified when they look into blue eyes. Lawrence possesses two that are as blue as a mountain lake. Some of the more primitive desert tribesmen thought there must be something superhuman about him because of this. On a second occasion an Arab was brought in charged with evil eye. Lawrence satisfied every one this time by simply looking intently at the man for about ten minutes. He almost seemed to hypnotize the tribesman. Then at the end of the ten minutes he announced that the evil eye had been driven off.

Lunch at Emir Feisal's headquarters was a more imposing event. The servants would bring in dish after dish of stewed thorn-buds, lentils, unleavened bread, and honey cakes. Of course the Arabs used their fingers, and Lawrence seemed to be as dexterous at this as the tribesmen. But Chase and I had not been there long enough to take such chances, and we used our own spoons. The drinking of tea and coffee is perhaps the most important ceremony connected with the meal. To show that you are enjoying it you must make as much noise as you can.

Dinner in the evening was much the same as lunch, but more extensive, and usually included a sheep whose throat had been cut while the butcher uttered a prayer in the name of Allah the Merciful and Compassionate. Then until late in the night Lawrence, Feisal, and the other leaders would discuss plans and occasionally exchange stories. Emir Feisal often added to the entertainment by telling of his adventures in days before the war when he and his family lived in Constantinople as prisoners of the Red Sultan, the bloodthirsty Abdul Hamid.

CHAPTER XIV

DESERT RAIDS AND TURKISH TRAIN WRECKS

AFTER the capture of Akaba, Lawrence saw ahead of him a far greater opportunity to help Britain and her Allies win the World War. His dream was to build up a still more formidable desert army, and to get the British government to send down enough supplies at least to help take care of that force until he and Allenby could drive the Turks out of Palestine and Syria; Lawrence had practically driven them out of Holy Arabia.

The officer in Cairo who took the greatest interest in the Arab War was General Clayton. Both Allenby and Clayton saw Lawrence was a genius, and they backed him to the limit, giving him a free hand. But to stage a great campaign, on the scale that young Lawrence now had in mind, involved a great deal more than simply rounding up a few thousand Arab warriors and dashing off to attack the Turks.

The desert nomads are a nervous people. They dearly love a scrap, and nothing delights them more than to swoop down in the night upon an enemy encampment; but having taken part in a fight, they then want to go off to an oasis, lie around under the palms, swap yarns about the great time they had, and talk about the next raid. When it is a question of capturing an enemy post or town and then settling down to the dull job of garrisoning the place, they lose all interest.

Lawrence's dream was to drive the Turks out of some forty or fifty square miles of territory. This meant a super-raid such as had not been staged in Arabia for nearly a thousand years. It also meant that the Arab forces would have to drive the Turks out of one region and then hold on to it while chasing them out of some other area;

so Lawrence saw he must really have two armies—one made up of regular troops on foot, and the other, of his irregular Bedouin warriors on their camels and horses. It would take nearly all of his time to look after the Bedouins, and so General Clayton sent down a regular army officer to organize an auxiliary infantry force. This was another Irishman, Lieutenant-Colonel P. C. Joyce. Joyce had been a soldier all his life, and had served through the Boer War and in Egypt and the Sudan. But, like Lawrence, he also was an adventurer at heart. Physically he was just the opposite of Lawrence, for while Lawrence stood barely five feet three, Joyce was an Irish giant of six feet three. As Lawrence remarked, "When Joyce mounts a camel, it looks like one mountain on top of another."

Surely there was no stranger regular army in the world than the one that Joyce organized. Nearly every man in it was a deserter from the Turkish army. The old Turkish Empire included most of the countries inhabited by Arabic peoples, and when Turkey joined Germany early in the World War several hundred thousand men of Arab blood were conscripted. But when Grand Sherif Hussein and his four sons launched the Arab revolt, the Arabic-speaking soldiers in the Turkish army heard about it, and large numbers of them began to desert. Their long training as infantrymen in the service of the sultan of Turkey made it possible for Joyce to build up a fairly well drilled force. But even these fellows had some of the care-free, playful habits of their wandering Bedouin relatives. For instance, they distinguished between corporals and sergeants in a rather unusual way. The corporals wore one wrist-watch, and the sergeants wore two.

Allenby also helped Lawrence by sending down an armored car section, consisting of a number of armored Rolls-Royce automobiles, with machine-guns in their turrets; they could race across flat stretches of desert at a speed of from fifty to seventy miles an hour. Allenby also provided Lawrence with a squadron of aëroplanes. This was partly in response to a plea that had been made to Lawrence by King Hussein. After the capture of Akaba, occasional German planes would swoop down over the Arab encampments, attempting to frighten the Bedouins with their strange devil birds, and also by dropping "eggs" that sometimes blew a few camels to bits. But instead of frightening the Arabs, this simply led them to insist that Lawrence get them some "fighting swallows" too. One day a royal courier arrived from Mecca and handed Lawrence a scroll on which was the following message:

> O faithful one! Thy government has aëroplanes as the locusts. By the grace of Allah, I implore thee to ask thy king to despatch us a dozen or so.
>
> HUSSEIN IBN ALI.

When the British airmen arrived they were obliged to wear Arab head-dress. In fact, every British officer was forced to do so, since the people of Holy Arabia look upon it almost as a crime to wear a European hat. But even then the airmen soon found that they would have to fly at a considerable height or get their planes shot full of holes by their playful Bedouin friends. The desert Arab can hardly keep from shooting at anything that is moving fast. They even used to pepper the armored cars. Then when they heard that this was wrong, they would come and make the most profuse and polite apologies.

When they were not out bombing the Turks, the British aviators used to spend some of their spare time taking the Bedouin sheiks for joy-rides. The commander of the aërial squadron was a young flier from Liverpool, Captain Harold Furness-Williams, and it was he who gave Sheik Auda Abu Tayi his first flip. Auda was the cheerful old brigand who had already shown his bravery by marrying twenty-eight wives.

One day, several weeks before the arrival of the British planes, a German aëroplane came over a Howeitat encampment. The tribesmen actually shot it down with their rifles, and then they ran out and clipped off its wings so that it would not fly away!

On one occasion Captain Furness-Williams flew from Akaba to Cairo. Before he left the Arab base-camp the rest of the fliers asked him to bring back as many bottles of refreshing drinks as his "bus" would carry. So before leaving Cairo he tied the bottles to various parts of the plane, in order to distribute the load. He took off without breaking a bottle. Off he flew, all the way across the wild mountains and desert of the Sinai peninsula. But when he came down on the flying field at Akaba, he made a bad landing, flopped the plane over on its back, and smashed every single bottle. His fellow-sufferers in that thirsty land were heartbroken when they saw the plane come in and turn over. They told the pilot that they would rather have seen his blood soaking into the sands than all that priceless liquid!

During the months while Colonel Joyce was organizing the regular army, and while the great supply depot at Akaba was being established, Colonel Lawrence devoted himself to winning more friends among the Bedouin tribes and to leading his camel-men on spectacular raids. But his chief pastime was blowing up trains. During the war Lawrence probably destroyed more enemy property than any one single man. He became the world's greatest train-wrecker. This was one of his ways of keeping his men supplied with food, and whenever he needed more flour or ammunition, he would go over and waylay a Turkish train on its way down from Damascus to Medina. It does seem strange indeed to think of a shy young Oxford graduate turning train-wrecker and leader of desert warriors on a hundred thrilling raids! One day Colonel Lawrence remarked to me there were few more interesting sights than to see a train-load of Turkish soldiers going into the air when a mine was set off. His little pastime of placing mines he called "planting tulips."

One evening he started off in the direction of the Turkish railway at the head of his column of picked brigands. As the camels ambled up the mountain gorge, the Arabs chanted weird war-songs, most of the verses in praise of Lawrence. After riding for two nights by moonlight, over a region almost as barren as any on this planet, the raiders arrived at a ridge of low hills where from the crest they could look down on the railway line. Lawrence gave a signal, and the Bedouins slid off the humps of their camels and left them at the foot of the hills, out of sight. For eight hours they crouched there watching the patrols that went up and down the line at regular intervals every two hours or so.

At midday, when he knew that the Turks would be taking their usual rest and siesta, Lawrence slipped down to the line alone, walking barefoot in order to leave as light impressions on the ground as possible. Picking out a spot he thought would be a good place for planting a tulip, he began digging a hole between the ties. It took him more than an hour, because he had to carry the earth in his robe, held up like an apron, for a distance of about a hundred and fifty feet, to where it would not excite suspicion. Then into the hole he placed an extra heavy charge of blasting gelatin and TNT. He put in far more than he usually planted, because he wanted to make quite sure of getting a train.

After setting his mine, pushing the detonators into the dynamite, and connecting the electric wires, he carefully filled in the rest of the hole with earth and when it was leveled he took a camel's-hair brush and artistically smoothed the ground until no one could tell it had been touched. Then he walked backward down the line for many yards, sweeping out his tracks with the camel's-hair brush and his robe, at the same time burying the wires. Leaving the line, he continued burying them until he was up the hillside several hundred yards away from the mine.

After a little while a train appeared, coming slowly around a bend. It was a mixed train with both freight and passenger cars. Guards were riding on top of the cars, and others were inside looking out through loopholes. When it drew near the fatal spot, the guards saw nothing more to arouse their suspicion than what appeared to be a lone Arab shepherd with his staff, squatting among the rocks.

Not until the front wheels of the engine had passed over his tulip did he touch it off. Then, as his Arabs lay just over the brow of the hill, waiting breathlessly, he sent the electric current into the gelatin. An enormous black cloud of smoke and dust arose. For a moment it shut off all view of the train. The roar of the explosion was like the crash of some great building collapsing from an earthquake. The engine was lifted bodily from the track and broken squarely in two.

The boiler exploded, and with a loud clatter a shower of iron and steel rose high in the air, many pieces coming down several hundred yards away. In addition to stores of food and ammunition, the train was carrying several hundred Turkish soldiers on their way to join the forces under General Fakhri Pasha in Medina. As they poured out of the train, the Arabs raked them with their rifle-fire from the rocks.

By this time a rumor had reached the Turkish army that a mysterious young Englishman was leading the Arabs, and the Turks and Germans had offered a reward of many thousands of dollars to any one who would capture Lawrence, dead or alive. Some of the Turkish officers apparently thought this might be the mystery man, and started toward Lawrence; but before they had covered many paces he whipped out his revolver and used it with such effect that there was little danger of his falling prisoner on that day. Lawrence was an excellent shot, with both revolver and rifle. In fact, there was no one in the Arab army who could excel him. None ever saw him practise, but he must have spent weeks and weeks at it, for he seldom missed a shot.

Most of the Turkish soldiers tumbled down behind the opposite railway embankment and began shooting out from between the coaches and between the wheels. But Lawrence had come ready for just this sort of thing. He had an Australian and an Englishman with him, one of whom used a machine-gun and the other a Stokes mortar. A few well placed shells from the Stokes made a shambles out of the crowd of Turks hiding behind the embankment. Those who were not killed by the bursting trench mortar shells got up and ran. Then they came into the line of fire of the Lewis gun.

The Arabs, seeing that they were masters of the situation now, jumped out from behind the rocks, dashed down to the train, and began looting it. They fairly went wild with joy; there is nothing that delights the hearts of desert warriors quite so much as an opportunity like this to make themselves temporarily rich. Sometimes they would quarrel over a mail-bag or a Turkish rifle; Lawrence would have to step in and settle the argument to keep one of them from being killed.

During the entire campaign, he dynamited seventy-nine Turkish bridges, as well as many trains. Upon one occasion he happened to blow up a train on which one of the principal Turkish generals, Djemal Pasha, was traveling, but there were so many soldiers aboard and the train was so heavily armed that Lawrence and his Bedouins had to be content with wrecking the train and sniping at the Turks.

So famous did Lawrence become as a train-wrecker that Turkish officers in Damascus willingly paid double price for seats in the last coach, because they had heard he nearly always touched off his tulips under the engine. He did this, of course, in order to prevent the engine from uncoupling and racing on to the next station for reinforcements.

Before the end of the campaign Lawrence had developed into a real expert in the use of high explosives. His skill at tulip planting became a byword, and after the final surrender of the Turkish army it was jokingly reported in Cairo that when he came through on his way home to London he intended blowing up the great bridge across the Nile, near British army headquarters, merely for sentimental reasons, in order to complete his record and end the war with an even eighty bridges!

Whenever Lawrence and the members of his body-guard captured a Turkish railway station along the line between Damascus and Medina, Lawrence would remove the station bell as a souvenir. Many of the bells now decorate the homes of his friends in England, along with a few Turkish metal mileposts. It was said in the East that Lawrence would capture a Turkish railway station merely to add another bell to his collection.

On nearly all his raids, Lawrence was accompanied by his personal body-guard, a

ABDULLAH, LEADER OF LAWRENCE'S BODY-GUARD

picturesque corps of picked men. He chose only two or three from each tribe. This meant that he had many blood-enemies serving in the corps, men who could never become very friendly with each other. Hence they were not likely to plot against him. Also, no matter where he went in Arabia he would always have a member of the corps who knew the region.

Every warrior in the desert wanted to belong to Lawrence's body-guard because its members had more opportunities for loot than any of the other troops. They spent most of their money on fine clothes, and when riding across the desert behind Lawrence they looked like a billowy Oriental flower-garden.

Of course, they were obliged to face danger oftener than any of the other fighting men, for Lawrence was always sending them on long and hazardous missions. When they all rode across the desert together, young Lawrence, dressed in his robes of pure white and mounted on his white she-camel, led the column. At each end of the cavalcade rode a desert poet. They improvised songs as they went. First one poet would sing out a verse, and then all of the other members of the body-guard would repeat it. Every one would wait for a moment or two, and the other poet would burst forth with a verse in reply. So on it went, back and forth. The verses were on all sorts of subjects, including King Hussein, their lady-loves, and Sidi (Lord) Lawrence.

"I wish he would pay us another five dollars a month!"

That, accompanied by rhetorical Arabic flourishes, would be the theme of one verse. Or again it would be:

"I wonder if Allah has seen the head-cloth which has the good fortune to cover our Lord Lawrence's head. It is not a good head-cloth, and he should give it me."

The truth was, however, that his head-cloths were as beautiful as any they had ever seen, and his playful "sons" wanted them.

Lawrence's lieutenant, who kept the members of the body-guard under a sort of wild discipline, was an undersized, fiery little Bedouin known as Abdullah the Pock-Marked. His face was a mass of little craters caused by a severe attack of smallpox. Abdullah was proud of the fact that he had fought in the service of nearly every prince of Arabia, and prouder still that he had been imprisoned by nearly every one of them. He was a dried-up little fellow, a great expert on the subject of camels, and absolutely fearless. If any member of the body-guard misbehaved he would give him a sound beating. Abdullah was greatly attached to Lawrence and wanted to accompany him everywhere that he went. On one occasion Lawrence took him across to Allenby's headquarters in Palestine. While Lawrence was consulting with a group of British generals, Abdullah wandered about the camp alone and was picked up and arrested as a suspicious character. He was so heavily armed that the British were afraid he had come in from the desert to assassinate somebody.

Several hours went by, and Lawrence was wondering what had happened to Abdullah the Pock-Marked. Then the telephone in Allenby's office rang, and the officer on duty at the guard-house said he had a fiery little Arab locked up there who claimed to be one of Sidi Lawrence's sons.

"We wish that this fellow Lawrence would come and get his brigand," said the voice over the wire, "because he is eating up all of the oranges at police headquarters."

Among the members of this *corps d'élite* were two picturesque Bedouin youths who were as inseparable as David and Jonathan, Ferraj and Daoud by name. When Lawrence and Abdullah got back from Allenby's headquarters, they found that the two lads had been locked up in the Akaba jail. When Lawrence demanded an explanation from Sheik Yussef, the Arab mayor of the town, Yussef laughed and swore, then laughed again. He said that he had a handsome, tall white camel, and that one night she strayed away. In the morning he heard a commotion out in the street. Opening the latticed window he heard the crowds in the bazaar roaring with laughter as they watched a camel that had blue legs and a red head. It was the mayor's favorite dromedary. A few minutes later Sheik Yussef found Ferraj and Daoud down on the beach trying to get the sea-water to take blue indigo and red henna off their arms and clothes.

"They denied all knowledge of the affair, but Allah will pardon me for doubting them," said the old sheik, as he slapped his thigh and roared again.

In the desert, life is lonely at best, and need for mutual protection calls for close friendship. Ferraj and Daoud were always together until there came to them the Destroyer of Delights and the Garnerer of Graveyards. Daoud died of a fever, whereupon Ferraj committed suicide by galloping headlong into the Turks.

CHAPTER XV

THROUGH THE LINES AS A SPY

DURING the months while he was waiting for the Arab regular army to be drilled and equipped, Lawrence also made several trips through the Turkish lines. On one occasion he disguised himself as an Arab woman, and on another he slipped around across the North Arabian Desert, came down upon one of the largest Turkish railway bridges in all Syria, blew it into the air with his tulips, and then vanished into the blue again.

To disguise himself as an outcast Arab woman was easy, because all he had to do was to put on a ragged dress and outer robe, completely cover his face with a veil, adopt a falsetto voice, and walk with the hip-swinging movement like all the Oriental women who carry burdens on their heads from childhood. But Lawrence was the only man in the Arab army, or on the entire Allied side during the war, who was able to penetrate through the Turkish lines dressed as a woman. The Turks rarely stopped one of the opposite sex. They considered it beneath their dignity to bother about a mere female. Besides, a woman's veil is a sacred garment in most Mohammedan countries, and no stranger is allowed to look upon a woman's face unless he is her father or brother or husband. In his disguise Lawrence visited many Turkish bases and even looked over their lines of trenches without being caught. He obtained a great deal of information which was important to his own army as well as to Allenby's forces in Palestine when the combined British and Arabian hosts launched their final drive to sweep the Turks out of Palestine and Syria in one of the most dazzling cavalry drives of all time.

Of course masquerading as a woman was none too easy, despite the Oriental veil that covered Lawrence's face. One afternoon when he was looking over the Turkish defenses at Amman, a city in the hills of Moab some fifty miles east of Jerusalem, a group of Turkish soldiers tried to flirt with him and followed him for nearly a mile, laughing and calling him playful names. Naturally he did not respond to their advances and got away as quickly as ever he could.

On his longest trip through the lines in disguise Lawrence accompanied a Bedouin sheik and posed as the old man's son. He could easily do this because he was so small, and his pink cheeks made him look like a mere lad.

The Turkish army occupied all of Syria at this time, but many of the Arab villagers were eager to rise up and start a revolt of their own, hoping to throw off the Turkish yoke immediately, as King Hussein and his sons and their followers had done farther south. When Lawrence visited their head men he cast aside his disguise and told them who he was. Of course they all knew about the great reward that had been placed on his head by the Turks and Germans. But no one attempted to betray him.

They had all heard about his prowess as a dynamiter of Turkish trains and bridges. So they begged him to show them how it was done. They said he could begin by blowing up anything that he liked in their neighborhood; provided, of course, it belonged to the Turks. In order to impress them and win their friendship so that he could depend on their joining the revolt a little later when his army advanced into Syria, he decided to destroy one of the largest steel and concrete bridges in all the Orient. This he did that very night.

The Syrian village Arabs with whom he was staying belonged to a tribe called the Metawileh. Accompanied by almost every man, woman, and child in the entire tribe, Lawrence went down to the Turkish railway line under cover of darkness and planted tulip after tulip under the ends of the bridge and under the great concrete columns that held it up. Then connecting the many charges to a single series of electric wires he went up the hillside for a short distance, called the Metawileh around him, and told them to look intently in the direction of the bridge. Of course this all seemed very mysterious to the ignorant tribesmen, and a moment later when Lawrence pulled the switch at his side they were stunned when they heard the roar. Many even threw themselves on the ground and covered their faces, believing they had heard a clap of thunder announcing the end of the world. The giant bridge went skyward in a mass of flame and smoke. Flames shot into the air for hundreds of feet.

Never had the Metawileh either seen or heard anything like this great explosion. To them it was all magic, and not only did they swear on the Koran to do whatever King Hussein or Emir Feisal commanded of them, but many were ready to fall down and worship this mysterious little man who had performed the greatest miracle in all their experience.

Before leaving Syria, Lawrence even went into Damascus, where the Turkish army had its headquarters. He knew that the governor, although outwardly on good terms with the Turks, was secretly an Arab sympathizer and was in fact of pure Arabic blood. So Lawrence slipped into the governor's house, dined with him, and spent the most of a night talking over the future and explaining to the governor that it would not be long now until the Arab army would reach Damascus. Of course Lawrence's fighting men were still hundreds of miles to the south. But he was confident that they were going to win the campaign, and sure that the famous old city of Damascus, which most of the Arabs regard as the earthly place nearest to paradise, would soon be an Arab capital again.

Before returning south to Arabia, Lawrence rode across most of the country, not only around Damascus, but also around

Deraa, a few miles farther south, the junction for all the Turkish railway lines in this part of the Near East. The observations that he made were most valuable to him a few weeks later when he commenced his spectacular advance north from Akaba.

But he had a narrow escape in Deraa. While walking through the bazaar, still posing as the son of the old sheik, he was seized by Turkish soldiers. They took him to headquarters, threw him on the floor before the commandant, and declared that he was a deserter. Every able-bodied Arab in the Turkish Empire was supposed to be in military service, helping the sultan and the kaiser fight the Allies. They had no idea that this stripling was the great Lawrence. So cleverly was he disguised that they were certain he was what he appeared to be, a young Bedouin from the desert. They gave him a terrific flogging with a cat-o'-nine-tails and beat him until he fainted. His back was frightfully bruised and torn. Then they threw him out into the street more dead than alive. The old sheik who had been with him had been forced to flee. Several hours later Lawrence regained consciousness; and, barely able to crawl, he made his way out of Deraa to an Arab encampment, under cover of night.

On his way south, still accompanied by the Arab sheik Dahmi, he had another close call. They had got as far south as the great oasis of Azrak, which lies deep in the desert to the southeast of Damascus. Here they were overtaken by a courier from Akaba with the news that Turkish spies had just arrived, along with a caravan of Syrian merchants, at the headquarters of the Arab army. Lawrence decided that there was no time to be lost and that he must get to Akaba immediately in order to give the spies his personal attention.

So Lawrence and Dahmi started on a forced ride across the desert, a ride that only a man of great endurance could have survived. But by now Lawrence had become such a veteran camel rider that there were few Arabs who could keep up with him for more than a day and a night. Lawrence had been making a careful study of the Arab camels, and those that he himself rode were the finest that he could buy from the central desert, where the fastest running camels are bred.

The camel is a rather mysterious animal and few Europeans ever learn how to handle him properly. There are two important types in the world: the camel with two humps, which is found to the north and east of Persia, chiefly in the Gobi Desert; and the one-humped camel of Arabia and the Sahara. The two-humped animal from Central Asia is slow and used only as a beast of burden. The one-humped camel, however, is a far different creature. The Greeks called him the dromedary, which was their word for a camel that runs. Some of the dromedaries in Central Arabia are trained to travel at high speed. Lawrence had many of his Bedouin warriors mounted on these racing camels and occasionally they would cross stretches of the desert at twenty-eight or thirty miles an hour. Of course they could not run at such speeds for a long time, but they could keep it up until they had easily outdistanced slower camels, and they were just the thing for use on a raid. When going at top speed their long legs shot out like huge pistons.

Ordinarily when jogging across country a camel caravan would travel at six or seven miles an hour, and on very long journeys the pace would be set at around five miles. On this run from Azrak to Akaba, a distance of nearly three hundred miles, Lawrence broke all records for camel riding in Arabia.

CHAPTER XVI

A RIP VAN WINKLE CITY

RECENTLY it has been reported from Cairo and Jerusalem that a fabulous cache of precious stones and ancient gold ornaments has been discovered by Arabs in one of the temples of a "Lost City" in Arabia. For hundreds of years the city has been uninhabited except for wandering Bedouins, who occasionally camp in the caves of the shelving rock, on their way to fresh oases and pastures new. A poor son of the desert while prowling about one of the desert temples of this deserted city is said to have stepped on a "moving stone." Before he knew what had happened the earth dropped from under him and the secret stone swung back into place. Like Ali Baba, the frightened Arab found himself in

THE ONLY ENTRANCE TO THE LOST CITY

a subterranean vault, but he was provided with no magic formula such as "Open sesame," to free him from his prison.

The Arab groped around in the dark until he found a passage. Crawling cautiously forward on his hands and knees to keep from plunging into an unexpected pit, he suddenly reached a great open chamber. He rubbed his eyes. He could not believe he was in the middle of an "Arabian Nights" tale. Scattered before him were precious stones and heaps of gold—pirates' gold of the dim dead days of Tyre and Sidon. The bewildered Arab, still thinking he was dreaming, had enough presence of mind to tie some of the jewels into his head-cloth before he continued to look for a means of escape from the underground cavern. At last he saw a gleam of daylight and escaped through a narrow opening in the red cliffs far above the place where he had stepped on the stone trap-door that had precipitated him into the secret treasure vault.

The jewels eventually reached the bazaars

of the Holy City. Archæologists who examined them were of the opinion that they dated from biblical antiquity. They may have enhanced the beauty of the Queen of Sheba when she paid her famous call on King Solomon, or perhaps they had been stolen from the palace of some Pharaoh of Egypt.

The reports are that this buried treasure is likely to surpass in value and equal in importance thc discoveries made by Lord Carnarvon and Howard Carter in the Valley of the Kings. If so it will be a great discovery. At any rate, an expedition from the British Museum started for the Lost City in the spring of 1927—just nine years after Chase and I had been there. We also looked for jewels, but we were not lucky enough to step on any moving stone!

It was in the very same cañon leading to this Lost City that Lawrence, the youthful military genius, led his Bedouins to a brilliant victory against the Turks on October 21, 1917.

It had been Lawrence's enthusiastic description of the faded flamingo palaces and temples carved out of the living rock that had fired me with a determination to see the city. Shortly after the Turko-Bedouin battle in this city of mystery and ghosts, I was fortunate enough to get Emir Feisal's permission to do a bit of wandering on my own among the so-called Enchanted Mountains of Edom.

Although not far from the coast, these red mountains are in an isolated and little known region.

A ninety-mile journey across mountain and desert brings you to the mysterious region of the Lost City. But unless you have a Bedouin guide you will have an extremely difficult time finding it, for it is hidden away in a pocket in the mountains.

Mounted on Emir Feisal's dromedaries, fleet racing camels, from the central Arabian Desert, Harry Chase and I set out from Akaba in the spring of 1918. Bouncing along beside us were some of his Sons of Ishmael whom he had assigned as our body-guard. Among them were several daredevils from Lawrence's famous corps of picked men. We also had a number of other men of Arab blood who came from various parts of the Near East and had little in common. Our first day's march took us up the furnace-like Wady Ithm, down which Lawrence had brought his desert hordes to the capture of the Turkish base at Akaba. This grim gorge resembles the famous Khyber Pass which connects India with Central Asia.

At first the members of our body-guard were as merry as a crowd of college men setting off for a football game, but on the second day they began to bicker and then to quarrel. Finally to keep them from shooting each other I cajoled them into letting me take the bolts out of their rifles, and I kept them in my saddle-bags after that. So for the remainder of the journey the Arabs made interesting traveling companions, but they were not worth much as a body-guard.

The region we passed through on our trek to the Lost City reminded me of the bad lands of the Dakotas and the barren mountains of Baluchistan and Afghanistan. On the evening of our first day out we crossed the ball-room-floor mud-flats and passed between the mighty red cathedral rocks of Rhumm which Lawrence describes so vividly in his "Revolt in the Desert." Some of the Turkish outposts were only a short distance away, but not a single skirmish with the enemy occurred to lend excitement to the expedition.

After several days of traveling while it was light, and camping beside water-holes at night, those precious oases which are a thousand times more important to the Arab than railroad junctions and gas stations to us, our caravan ascended a steep winding track and came out on a high plateau. We were nearing the goal of our journey. Before us spread the Enchanted Mountains of Edom, the great wall of red and white peaks that guard the approach to what is perhaps the loveliest and least known of all the ancient cities of the East.

Some twenty miles to the north of us lay that desolate and sunken region, the lowest on the face of the earth, the Valley of the Dead Sea. On our right, melting into cloudy purple and gray, lay the vast desert of Central Arabia and, somewhere in it, two strips of glistening steel, the "Pilgrims' Railway" connecting Damascus with Medina, the Turkish line where Lawrence planted those tulips of his and blew up trains and bridges.

Straight ahead were the sacred mountains of the ancient land of Edom, a towering range of seemingly impenetrable sandstone through which we must pass to reach the Lost City we had come to see. Directly below us was a steep rocky slope by which we must descend. One of our Arabs pointed to a valley down there, which was many miles wide, though from where we were it looked like a *cul-de-sac*. After several hours, during which we were forced to lead our slipping and stumbling dromedaries, we came to what seemed to be the end of the valley. Then rounding a huge mass of white sandstone we found ourselves entering a narrow chasm, a mere rift in the massive mountain wall. From a width of twelve miles our valley had narrowed down to a mere crack of twelve feet, with its walls towering hundreds of feet above us. Through this Sik, as the Arabs call the precipitous gorge, our horses and camels scrambled and stumbled, clambering over huge boulders and pushing through thickets of oleanders. Lizards slithered across the stones, and our companions amused themselves by popping at them with their pistols. The narrow chasm seemed to grow wilder and more impressive with every step. Hassan Kalil told us that we were in the rent in the rock that appeared when Moses smote these desolate mountains with his rod and brought forth a gushing stream for his thirst-maddened followers on their way toward the Promised Land of Canaan. Here was a mighty crack in the mountains, and here danced a sparkling brook; who were we to question Hassan's story?

High overhead wheeled an eagle, as if it were the reincarnation of an ancient king of Edom watching our caravan approaching the desert streets of the sleeping capital. The morning sun warmed the rocks, transforming them into an old master's soft red. At times the Wady Musa, or Valley of Moses, became so narrow that we could sit on our camels, and reach out and touch the walls on either side. The stratified rocks rose above us to such heights that at times they almost shut out the sky. Dark walls there were, where no ray of the sun could ever penetrate. It was like a Grand Cañon of the Colorado in miniature—but more colorful and more exquisite.

After an hour we suddenly rounded a sharp bend. Before us was a sight that fairly took our breath away, and even the Arabs stood still in awe and bewilderment. There stood a Grecian temple of delicate limpid rose. At a glance you thought it shaped of the stuff of which dreams are made. But it was real, for here the Praxiteles and Michelangelos of a bygone day had carved this lovely structure from the mountain wall. And what an eye for the dramatic those masters of old must have had! To get their effects and to carve the temple from the cliffs of Edom they used a toothed tool. The multicolored strata seemed to swirl like watered silk, and at the hour of our arrival the morning sun fell full on the temple, while we stood in the gloom of the narrow gorge that is the only entrance to this city whose very name has been lost to history.

In the whole world no other abode of men has such an effective gateway as this Rip Van Winkle city in far-off Arabia. The Greeks called it Petra, which is their word for rock, and that is the name by which we know it to-day. The ancient Hebrews called it Sela, their word for rock. But what its original name was no mortal knows.

Of a corrupt Greco-Roman style, the

first temple had been carved from the cliff about two thousand years ago, during the days when the legions of Rome penetrated to this region in the desert, about the time of Hadrian, A. D. 131. Hassan Kalil from the depth of his knowledge, or perhaps error, told me that it was called El Kazneh (the treasury), because it holds a treasure. High up above the great columns is a giant urn, and this the Arabs believe is filled with the gold and precious stones of the Pharaohs. In the past, doubtless ever since the tradition came into being, they have tried vainly to crack the urn. But it is of solid stone and defies them. It has been chipped by thousands of bullets, and after I had returned their rifle-bolts to them my men also opened fire, trying to burst open the "treasury of the Pharaohs." Apparently they did no more damage than their predecessors.

What god or goddess was worshiped in the carving of that exquisite art? In the opinion of Colonel Lawrence, who has been there many times, the temple was dedicated to

Isis, the Egyptian goddess, whose cult in the time of the reign of Hadrian had spread throughout the Mediterranean countries. The shadow of the Goddess of the Nile seems to brood over the curving lines and tints of this cameo at the mouth of the Valley of Moses. Could this Temple of Isis be the one mentioned in the despatch telling of the Bedouin's stepping on the "moving stone" that precipitated him into the treasure-room? Perhaps the light-hearted and irresponsible marksmen in my body-guard were not quite so foolish as I had imagined when they talked of the temple's hidden treasure. Chase and I may have stood within a pace or two of that same moving stone!

CHAPTER XVII

THE WONDERS OF THE LOST CITY

THE city itself lay a few hundred yards farther on in an oval basin, a gigantic excavation wrought by the forces of nature. From the nine-thousand-foot plateau on which we stood when we first beheld the mountains of Edom, we had now dropped to an altitude of a thousand feet. The main streets, in the days when the city teemed with life, lay in the bottom of this basin, while in the encircling cliffs were hundreds of temples, palaces, and tombs, all carved from the rock in the same manner as the Temple of Isis. These remain unchanged by the passing hand of time.

The colors of Petra have been the marvel of every traveler who has found his way through the rent in the eastern wall of these mountains. The sun's rays transform the sandstone cliffs into rainbows of rock. From the narrow strata flash out layers of vermilion, saffron, orange, pink, and white. At sunset they glow with an eerie radiance before sinking into the blackness of the desert night. We took autochrome pictures to preserve the exact colors, and we even brought away samples of the strata in our saddle-bags.

Rock-carved stairways, some more than a mile in length, lead to the tops of many of the mountains around Petra. Most of them lead to ancient high places, sacrificial altars where the people worshiped thousands of years ago. We ascended one that brought us out nearly a thousand feet above the city. Another led to a temple now called El Deir (the Convent). Its rose-red façade is carved, cut, and hewn from the cliff to a height of a hundred and fifty feet. At the top is another gigantic urn which the Arabs say is also full of jewels. But it would take a genie to reveal the secret of the urn.

Another stairway led up to a Mount of

Sacrifice, an isolated peak dominating the whole basin. Lawrence considered the place of worship on this pinnacle as the best existing example of an ancient Semitic high place. There are two altars, one hollowed out for fires, the other with a blood-pool to receive the blood of the victims offered to Dhu-shara and Allat, chief god and goddess of ancient Petra in the days when the city was known by some other name that has long since vanished from the pages of history. Near the altar are two tall obelisks, used in the strange worship which was prevalent in those bygone days.

Behind the Mount of Sacrifice was a second and slightly loftier peak surmounted by the crumbling remains of a crusader's castle, and we wondered what knights lived here and where they came from. Probably they too were beauty worshipers from France or England who left home in search of adventure and then ended their days on this remote height in Edom.

Further off loomed a black mountain. It

was crowned with a white dome that glistened in the desert sunlight like a bleached skull. The Arabs say that Aaron, leader of the wandering Israelites and brother of Moses, was borne here and buried. At any rate tradition has it that this is Mount Hor. That white dome is a part of the tiny mosque and a tomb which the Bedouins have built to mark the burial-place of one who is a great prophet in their eyes.

We climbed Mount Hor, with a blistering sun blazing down on the barren rocks. It was too steep for our camels and horses, and the merciless heat of the Arabian noon seemed to shrivel us to the size of the lizards that were the only living things we saw. As we lay panting on the summit we peered through a knot-hole in the heavy wooden door and there saw a Turkish flag still flying over Aaron's tomb. Apparently we were the first to scale this treeless mountain since the war in far-off France had extended its battle-line across the world to the foot of Mount Hor.

Everywhere in these forgotten valleys we found palaces and temples of worship. The peoples of ancient Petra must have been just as religious and far more artistic and skilful than their successors who followed the standard of Mohammed. As we wandered from one temple to another it seemed as if in any one of them a wandering Arab might stumble upon the path to secret caverns and treasures.

It was not until a little more than a century ago that John Lewis Burckhardt, a Swiss traveler, disturbed the slumber of this Rip Van Winkle city. While wandering in the Near East, Burckhardt heard rumors of a city of rock lying on the fringe of the Arabian Desert. At last he found his way to that same narrow gorge and later returned to civilization with the news that he had been to this "rose-red city, half as old as time," which had not been mentioned in any literary record for more than a thousand years—not since A. D. 536. Since Burckhardt wrote of his adventure—and it was indeed an adventure, for he had to visit the city in Arab disguise, with the imminent possibility of being put to death by fanatics if discovered—not many travelers or archæologists have remained long enough to explore Petra. Not many have cared to remain long and run the risk of being picked off by Bedouin snipers hiding in the fastnesses of Edom.

The few Westerners who have been fortunate enough to venture into that narrow gorge and wander through the deserted streets, entangled with laurels and oleanders and carpeted with wild geraniums and poppies, have been struck with the decayed grandeur and elusive beauty of the city of ghosts. The Sik, or Wady Musa, when Petra was at its height, must have been the most fascinating thoroughfare in the world, running as it does between towering crags and toppling walls. At the height of its prosperity and importance, when the bells of camel caravans tinkled and chariots rattled between those towering sandstone cliffs, even the sophisticated and blasé Romans must have been amazed as they came out of the gorge and beheld the majestic buildings carved from these mountain walls.

No one knows who carved those lovely entrances, those matchless façades of rose-colored sandstone. No one even knows for certain whether the chambers to which they lead were actually places of worship. Indeed no one knows who were the earliest builders of Petra. It was an old city when the Israelites fled across the Red Sea before the chariots of the Pharaoh of the Exodus.

The story goes that when the Children of Israel were wandering in the wilderness they came upon this great city and asked permission to enter and refresh themselves. But the Petræans turned them from their doors and closed that narrow valley of approach to them. Thereupon the angry prophets of Israel, marshaling their well known curses, predicted the destruction and desolation of the city. But Petra was the capital of the Edomites, who in a friendlier epoch joined forces with the Israelites and Philistines against the Assyrians, and even in those days the city enjoyed a lucrative commerce with Judah, Israel, and Damascus. Before the fall of Jerusalem many of the Jews who fled from impending disaster and the ruthless legions of Titus sought refuge in Petra.

The Nabatæans, an ancient Arab tribe, conquered Edom and by 100 B. C. had created a powerful kingdom, extending north to Damascus, west into Palestine, and far into Central Arabia. The Nabatæans attained a high degree of culture and were celebrated for their glasswork, purple and fine linen, and pottery. Lawrence told me that they were stout old pirates, who frequently swooped down on the African coast and made devastating raids on the Sudan. Both King Solomon and the Queen of Sheba employed the Nabatæans. These people must have been the big business men of the ancient world, for they made their metropolis the center of a flourishing caravan traffic extending from Jerusalem, Damascus, Palmyra, and Babylon to Egypt and south to ancient Sanna. Petra had long had commercial and intellectual affiliations with Egypt. The old kings of Edom married into the families of the Egyptian Pharaohs. Much of the rock sculpture shows Egyptian influence. The gilded youth of Petra undoubtedly traveled to Egypt to put the finishing touches on their higher education.

The Greeks were familiar with this city, impregnable as a fortress in its mountains. Alexander the Great, who shed his storied tears when he ran out of worlds to conquer, really had an even better reason for weeping than history tells us. Petra was the one place in the world that he was unable to conquer. In his time the Nabatæans were still a virile race, and Petra, their capital, was at the zenith of its glory during the fourth century before Christ. Alexander sent an army to take the city, but it never got through the narrow gorge. The city did, however, succumb to Greek influence, and with its amphitheaters and palaces, its mystic groves and high priestesses of exotic religions, its hospitality to artists and philosophers, and its luxuries begotten by commerce, it became a Mecca for tourists. Petra was to Asia Minor what Rome and Athens were to Europe, and as a caravan center it served as the Chicago of the ancient world.

The prosperity of the rose-red city awakened the envy of the world-greedy Romans. Trajan sent one of his generals to conquer it in A. D. 105 and created the Roman province of Arabia Petræa. Under the Roman peace of the sword the city continued to be a flourishing center of caravan trade between Arabia, Persia, India, Egypt, Palestine, and Syria. But when Rome's power declined Petra also declined and finally languished, a forgotten city of vanishing memories, because no Homer or Virgil had immortalized its regal history. The Crusaders built many castles in the neighborhood in the twelfth century, but Saladin finally expelled the knights of the church from the entire peninsula of Arabia. Petra once more lapsed into its Rip Van Winkle sleep.

CHAPTER XVIII

A BATTLE IN A CITY OF SHADOWS

AS Chase and I strolled through the echoing streets it seemed as though the shadows of all those centuries hovered around, and yet it was not the ancient memories that were the most beguiling. I saw here the background of the battle that Lawrence had described to me so vividly a short time before. His was the first battle fought in Petra for seven hundred years. The Crusaders, stalking in armor, were the last previous warriors to sally out to fight in that basin and in the ribbon-like gorge.

Lawrence and his Arabs had captured the strategic port of Akaba, compelling the surrender of the Turkish garrison. The Turks realized that they must either recapture that exceedingly important post or reconcile themselves to the loss of Arabia. Petra commands the only practicable approach to Akaba through the Wady Ithm. Its possession was essential to the capture of Akaba. Lawrence was well aware of these strategic considerations, and based his plans on the topographical difficulties the Turks would have to encounter. The Wady Ithm is one of the most formidable passes in the world, and so Djemal Pasha, commander-in-chief of the Turkish armies in Syria, as the first step on the way to Akaba, ordered an attack on Petra with an infantry brigade, a crack cavalry regiment, and several organizations of light artillery. Three columns, supported by artillery and German aëroplanes, were to converge on Petra on October 21, 1917.

For the first time in centuries, dead and forgotten Petra throbbed with life. There, behind the gigantic ramparts that had defied Alexander the Great, Lawrence waited with his little Bedouin army. Camp-fires burned on the old altars of the gods, and on the ancient high places sentinels watched for the coming of the Turk. In the stone-hewn chambers of the tombs the Arabs sat in circles, telling their long stories and singing their songs, while the echoes resounded in the hollow spaces. Lawrence picked princely quarters for himself—the rose-tinted Temple of Isis at the entrance of the gorge. His archæological mind might have conjured priestesses and dancing-girls of Isis to dance for him, but on the subject of women he preferred a more prosy if not less extraordinary course of action. To the Sheik Khalil of Elgi, a neighboring village, he said he wanted all the able-bodied women of the district to be recruited and brought to Petra. They were to reinforce his troops and fight their part in the coming battle.

The women of the desert knew nothing about Red Cross work or canteen service, but they have always taken a personal share in the endless wars of their tribes. In skirmishes and blood-feuds they are often in the rear, urging their men on with shrill cheers and shouts of praise. They chant songs of storied paladins of the desert and shriek words of blame and elaborate curses if their men do not dash forward to the attack with sufficient boldness and gallantry. They all know how to handle rifles. The Bedouin women of the vicinity of Petra waxed enthusiastic over the idea of themselves taking an active part in a battle. Their butter-making and weaving were abandoned for the while, and, under the leadership of Sheik Khalil's wife they filed to Lawrence's headquarters in the rose-red Temple of Isis, as formidable and disheveled looking an army of Amazons as you could want to see. They were barefooted, dressed in long blue cotton robes, and wore golden bracelets on their arms and rings in their ears and noses.

Lawrence's plan was neat and effective. He remembered the stout defense the old Nabatæan kings put up when the army of Alexander attempted to capture Petra. The gorge was so narrow that only a few Turks and Germans could march through abreast.

He intrusted to the women the task of holding back the advancing column. They were stationed at the mouth of the gorge, near the Temple of Isis, there to cover the approach with rifles. The women, in their warlike frenzy, needed little coaching. They placed themselves in ambush behind rocks, behind the pillars of the temple, some of them with their half-grown children beside them, and awaited the fray.

The men were used as a mobile force with which to spring the jaws of a trap. Lawrence commanded the battle through the medium of a group of Bedouin youths whom he had picked for their speed as runners. They carried his messages swiftly from one detachment to another. He had only two mountain-guns and two machine-guns.

The first stage of the battle was a defense of the wide entrance to the gorge. With his meager forces Lawrence held his position for six hours and killed sixty Turks, with practically no casualties on his side. The Turks then stormed straight up the ridge with their whole force in spite of the steady fire of the Arabs. Lawrence vacated his position and split his force into two halves. These he sent to lie in ambush, each on one side of the valley just where it narrows and becomes a mere cleft through the mountain wall.

The Turks, thinking they had totally defeated Lawrence's force and that Lawrence had retired hurriedly into Petra, stormed into the valley and on into its narrowest part. A thousand were wedged there between the perpendicular walls of stone. When he gave the word, one of his aides fired a rocket into the air as the signal to attack. Pandemonium broke loose in the mountains of Edom. The Arabs poured a storm of fire into the rear of the Turkish column. The front of the column encountered the rifle-fire of the female brigade around the Temple of Isis. Other women and scores of children rolled boulders over the edges of the cliffs and on to the heads of the Turks and Germans. The column trapped in the gorge fell into a panic.

The sun was sinking behind the rose-colored mountains. Lawrence and his gallant lieutenant, Malud Bey, sent up a second rocket.

And now crouching figures were springing up from behind the rocks and leaping forward. "Allah! Allah!" The Bedouins swept down the ridges into the valley, while the rifle-fire of the women at the other end of the gorge became even more violent than before.

Lawrence's Arabs captured the entire Turkish transport, a complete field-hospital and hundreds of prisoners. Holy Arabia was saved.

After that epic fight the forgotten city was left once more to its abandoned quiet of centuries, but now a wandering Bedouin has fallen upon a hoard of hidden treasure. Perhaps he is one of the defenders of the desert who fought with Lawrence that day.

CHAPTER XIX

LAWRENCE BECOMES A BEDOUIN

NED LAWRENCE not only was a scholar and a fighter; he was also an actor. If he had not been one he never would have succeeded in gaining the confidence of the desert tribesmen in the amazing way that he did. It is no easy thing for a Westerner to go into a wholly Oriental country and live as Orientals do without occasionally giving the game away by behaving as a European. The Arabs are very suspicious, especially those who live in the Hedjaz, or Holy Arabia. They do not want Europeans in their country. In fact most of them think it just as terrible for a person of another religion to tread on the sacred soil of their holy country as we would consider it if unclean animals were admitted to one of our churches. For centuries they have held to this attitude. As a result they now carry it to fanatical lengths; and many a Christian who has penetrated Holy Arabia, beyond the few coast ports where they are allowed to trade, has been killed by the Arabs.

Lawrence knew that his every move was watched by the tribesmen. He knew they would be far more likely to work happily at his side if he paid them the compliment of dressing and living exactly as they do. So in the desert he wore only Arab garb. In traveling across the desert it is necessary to get along without luggage. Lawrence had nothing in his camel-bags excepting an extra white *abba* and an extra head-cloth or two, a few chunks of unleavened bread, a bar or two of chocolate to nibble on while riding, a large canteen to drink out of between wells, chlorine tablets to help purify water that would otherwise be undrinkable, a tooth-brush, a safety-razor, and a favorite book or so.

He also had his rifle, revolver, and ammunition. This rifle, by the way, had quite a record. It was of British make but had been captured by the Turks during the disastrous campaign at the Dardanelles when the Allies failed to break through to Constantinople. Enver Pasha, one of the three dictators who ruled Turkey during the war, had a specially inscribed gold plate set in its stock. In 1916, before the Turks suspected that the Arabs might revolt, he presented it to Emir Feisal. In it he had engraved these words: "To Feisal with Enver's regards." He told Feisal it was a token that the Turks had already won the World War! Later Enver was assassinated in Bokhara. I wonder if he ever knew to what use that rifle was put in the years that followed. Feisal presented it to Lawrence, who carried it on all of his raids. Every time he shot a Turk he cut a notch in the stock, big notches for officers, little ones for ordinary soldiers. After the war Lawrence presented it to the king of England.

In time the Arabs came to trust Lawrence as implicitly as they did their own leaders.

But he most certainly could not have won them over had he not completely mastered all the little everyday customs of the desert nomads. As an illustration of the importance the Arabian people place on little things, on one occasion another British officer went a short way into the desert with Lawrence. They spent the night in the tent of a Howeitat chief. The Englishman was waved to a place of honor on the guest-rug, but instead of tucking his feet under him and squatting Arab fashion he sat down as any Westerner might, with his feet stretched out in front of him. To the Arab this is as offensive as it would be for us to put our feet on the table at a dinner-party. So the officer was never popular with the Bedouins.

In Akaba I met a sheik who had a long scar across his face. When I asked Lawrence if it was a sword-slash received in battle, he laughingly replied:

"No, indeed. Several years ago that fellow was dining in the black goats'-hair tent of Ibn Rashid, an emir who rules over a region of the Central Arabian Desert between Palestine and Mesopotamia. Ibn Rashid's huge copper tray, filled with rice and gravy with chunks of mutton on top, had been placed in the center of the tent. The guests moved forward, and each got down on one knee in a circle around the feast. Each rolled back his right sleeve, and murmuring, 'In the name of God the merciful, the loving-kind,' they plunged their hands into the dish. After that no word was spoken. Each man gave himself over to the devouring of food. So greedy was this sheik that he choked on a lump of goat. To the Arab this is a disgrace. The fellow was so mortified at his breach of etiquette that he jerked out his knife and slit his mouth right up to the carotid artery in his cheek, just to show his host that the mishap was unavoidable because some meat had actually stuck fast in his back teeth."

To choke is a sign of bad breeding in Arabia. It not only indicates that you are greedy but that the devil has caught you in the act of trying to devour more food than you really should have. The nomad tribesmen of the desert never use knives and forks. They eat only with their hands. But it is an inexcusable breach of etiquette to eat with your left hand.

Nor will a Bedouin excuse a stranger merely because he is ignorant of their customs. If you are not familiar with their ways you are an outsider, and they feel hostile toward you.

It is also a sign of bad breeding if you fail to know the full family history of every Bedouin you meet. The reason for this is obvious. The population of the desert is not very great, and few nomads ever wander many hundreds of miles away from their own region. So they are obliged to know the complete family history of all with whom they come in contact because of the bitter blood-feuds between tribes and even between families. You must know that one man's father has been hanged. You must know that his mother was a divorced wife of some particular sheik, for it would be as awkward to ask about a man's father if he had been a famous fighter as it would be for us in this country to introduce a divorced woman to her former husband.

In order always to play safe Lawrence avoided asking direct questions of the Arabs. When he wanted information he would get it indirectly by cleverly leading the camp-fire talk to the subject in which he was interested. On one occasion he attended a war conference of the Arab sheiks in Emir Feisal's mud palace at Akaba. The chiefs were all squatting in a semicircle in the courtyard. Among them were six sheiks of the Ibn Jazi Howeitat. Lawrence was squatting in a corner where he could see the door. Suddenly I saw a look of anxiety come over his face. Leaping to his feet he hurried out of the courtyard, and I saw him engaging another group of Arabs in conversation and then walking off with them. That evening he told me why he had left the conference in such a hurry. He said the warriors who had been about to enter were relatives of old Auda Abu Tayi, the Bedouin Robin Hood. For several generations the two branches of the Howeitat tribe had been blood-enemies. Auda and a number of his followers were there conferring with Emir Feisal, and if the Ibn Jazi Howeitat sheiks had not been headed off there surely would have been a bloody battle in front of the emir. Incidents of this sort were happening constantly, and often it was only Lawrence's eagle eye and tact that prevented the Arab forces from breaking up and starting war on each other.

The old desert law of "an eye for an eye, and a tooth for a tooth" still holds good. If a member of one tribe happens to kill a member of another, it usually results in a blood-feud that involves all the relatives on both sides. Lawrence had many blood-enemies facing each other in his own bodyguard. But he usually managed to keep them at peace. On one occasion when he and his picked corps were raiding a Turkish railway station, one group tried to smash the door, and another pounded at the windows with their rifle-butts. One Arab clambered through a window. A moment later some one in the group outside the door thoughtlessly fired a bullet. When the door gave way the poor fellow was found dead. The man who had fired the shot dashed out of the station, jumped on his horse, and galloped off into the desert. He was in a hurry too, because he knew that several of the relatives of the dead man were in the bodyguard, and the law of the desert would make it necessary for them to shoot him if they got the chance. Sometimes it is possible to prevent the outbreak of a tribal blood-feud after such an incident. This can only be arranged if the relatives of the victim are willing to accept money damages instead of payment in blood. In this case the other members of Lawrence's corps all contributed and gave the relatives a hundred pounds in gold, which satisfied them. The man who had been shot happened to be something of a scalawag, and his own relatives only valued his life at about one hundred pounds (five hundred dollars).

The hospitality of the true desert Arab is well known. Once a traveler enters the part of Arabia occupied by a tribe, its members will neither injure nor kill him—provided he behaves himself. This is an unwritten law of the desert. They will not let him come to harm even if he happens to be an enemy; instead they will give him the best that they have. But this hospitality only lasts about three days, at the end of which time the stranger had better be on his way; that is, of course, unless he knows that he is among friends.

During the entire campaign Lawrence only met with one case of treachery against himself. It was when he was on a trip behind the Turkish lines and in a part of the desert inhabited by the Beni-Sakr nomads who were helping the Turks. Lawrence boldly went to their desert encampment and tried to win them over to the cause of the Arab revolt. Of course the sheiks of the Beni-Sakr all knew that the Turks and Germans had both offered great rewards for the capture of this young, fair-haired European—dead or alive. So one sheik broke the unwritten law of the desert, and while Lawrence was in his tent he sent a courier to the Turks to let them know that the man they wanted was there. Instinctively Lawrence knew something was in the wind, and he slipped away before the Turks had time to take him. Despite the fact that the Beni-Sakr looked upon Lawrence as their enemy, they gave their own treacherous sheik a cup of poisoned coffee. He had disgraced them, and he had to pay the penalty according to the desert code.

Here is an interesting way by which you can save your life if you are ever caught by a band of Arab brigands, and it is about the only way: If an Arab has you on the ground and is about to slit your throat, if you say the magic word *dakhilak* he will drop his dagger. The word means, "I have taken refuge with you," or in other words, "I am in your tent and at your coffee-hearth as your guest." This is an admission that you have completely surrendered to him and that you are pleading for mercy. The desert tribesmen rarely use this word, but when they do it conveys a sacred obligation.

The nomad Arab is in many ways a fine sportsman. He is a lover of personal liberty, and he is a poet. On the other hand the villagers and townsmen are often dirty, lazy, and not to be trusted. A townsman will show his respect for an Arab leader by kissing his hand. But no true warrior of the desert will do this. He considers it undignified and beneath him. He is as good as any man. To be sure, he is a bandit. But that is no disgrace, for it is one of the chief occupations of those who live in the desert. The Bedouin will rob any one. But he will seldom add abuse to the deed. The true Arab belongs to a race that has been highly civilized for thousands of years. They had a highly developed literature and philosophy when the inhabitants of Northern Europe and the British Isles were still in a savage state.

Both the regular and the irregular fighting men in the Arabian army received their monthly wages much the same as did all other troops who took part in the World War. But the Arabs, who have no coins of their own, use as their medium of exchange the Turkish five-dollar gold piece and the British sovereign, which is worth about the same amount. Lawrence succeeded in getting the British government to supply him with large quantities of gold, and he nearly always had a bag or two hanging from his camel saddle. His manner of paying off the Arabs was certainly different and far more picturesque than the methods used in the British, French, and American armies. Whenever a Bedouin sheik came in and hinted that perhaps Lawrence might like to make him a present, the colonel would point to the large bag of gold in one corner of the tent and tell him to help himself. He allowed each sheik to keep all that he could take out of the bag in one handful. One day a six-foot Howeitat giant opened the tent-flap and silently squatted on one of Lawrence's Baluchi rugs. After a cup of coffee and a cigarette he spoke. In the flowery language of a true desert orator he reminded Lawrence of the help he had been giving in the recent fighting. When Lawrence told his guest that he would indeed be honored if the sheik would put his hand into the bag of gold and see how much he could pick up with one hand, the tall Howeitat chieftain broke all records. He picked up exactly one hundred and forty-three gold sovereigns, the equivalent of $715! After that Lawrence was more cautious whenever this sheik turned up.

Sidi Lawrence's "Sons" were like children in some ways. They were particularly fond of such things as wrist-watches, field-glasses, revolvers, and trinkets of all kinds. There are few things the Bedouin admires more than generosity. To him it is a quality second only to bravery. Lawrence brought them caravans laden with presents rich and rare. His generosity even surpassed the stories that the Arab troubadours recounted in their songs around the camp-fires. He kept most of his gold at his base-camp near the head of the Gulf of Akaba. A Major T. H. Scott, of the Inniskilling Fusiliers, looked after the gold. He had it piled up in wooden boxes in one corner of his tent. As the guardian of these "golden goblins" Scott had a comical little dog hardly any bigger than a squirrel. He called it his Bulgarian weasel-hound. Even its bark was too feeble and squeaky to frighten off a robber at night. The Arabs knew where the gold was kept, but they were too faithful to Colonel Lawrence to disturb it. But old Auda Abu Tayi and a few of his companions did loot the supply depot a few times.

Whenever Lawrence wanted any gold he would drop into Scott's tent and remark:

"I think I'll do a little shopping."

Scott would ask him how many sovereigns he needed, and if Lawrence replied that twenty thousand would do (a hundred thousand dollars), Scott would pour the gold out on to a canvas in the middle of the tent and put it in little bags. Then Lawrence would send members of his bodyguard for it. Throwing it across their saddles the little band of picked men headed by the blond leader would ride off into the blue. He never even gave a receipt for all the gold he took from Akaba.

Lawrence usually gave his men from fifty to one hundred rounds of ammunition every day. And they shot it off into the air, no matter whether there was any fighting or not! If a soldier did such a thing in the American or British army he would be court-martialed. But the wild Bedouins blazed away at every bird they saw, even at wheeling vultures so high up in the sky that they were completely out of range. One afternoon a false rumor reached us at Akaba that a part of Feisal's army, led by

General Nuri Bey, had captured the important Turkish stronghold at Ma'an. Immediately the Arabs began a wild celebration. Thousands of rifles were fired off into the air. If the desert tribesmen who came into Akaba happened to see me walking along the sandy shore carrying a riding-crop or a cane they would shake their heads, stroke their beards, and say, "That fellow's mad!" But if Chase or I went about with a rifle, banging at every rock or sparrow in sight, the Bedouins would say to each other in Arabic, "These foreigners are not such silly fellows after all."

Chase and I had taken a supply of tinned food along to Arabia. One day we handed a can of beef to each of the Arabs in our personal body-guard. They did not seem eager to take it, and we afterward learned the reason for their uneasiness. They were afraid it was unholy. One of their religious customs is to repeat a prayer whenever they slaughter an animal for food. At the moment that an Arab sticks his knife into the throat of a sheep he utters the words: "In the name of Allah the Merciful and Compassionate!" When they opened our cans of meat they repeated this same prayer, fearful lest Messrs. Armour and Swift of Chicago had failed to do so.

I recall one morning in particular, a morning when Chase nearly got us into trouble. It was the same morning that we found a scorpion in Chase's blankets when he crawled out of his sleeping-bag. Chase was unlucky in that respect; every scorpion, centipede, snake, and flea in Arabia seemed to have a grudge against him. Well, on this morning, Chase handed a can of bacon to one of the members of our body-guard. He had brought it all the way from Cairo and saved it as long as he could. As he had had little to eat the night before, Chase brought out the bacon in anticipation of a real feast. But he ended by frying it himself. As soon as the can was opened the Bedouin cook dropped it like a hot coal and backed away shuddering with horror. His Moslem nostrils had been insulted by the smell of unclean and unholy meat. Like all Mohammedans, the Bedouins never use pork in any form. They do not even use lard. Instead they cook their food in butter made from goats' milk.

There was one picturesque young Bedouin who had the reputation of being the jolliest fellow in the army. His name was Ali Ibn Hussein. He was a reckless impertinent youth of nineteen and an unqualified outlaw. One of the requirements for membership in Lawrence's body-guard was the ability to leap on the back of a running camel with a rifle in one hand. Ali could do this easily, and he was reputed to be the fastest runner in the desert. Whenever he went into battle he always stripped off all of his clothes, down to his drawers. He laughingly said that it was the cleanest way to get wounded. Emir Feisal's father, King Hussein, was a strong-willed and rather tyrannical monarch. Most of the Arabs were afraid of him, but not so Ali. He would even tell wild jokes in the king's presence. Instead of wearing his hair in the usual scraggly fashion he had it plaited so that it hung in braids. He said he did this in order to encourage lice to live in it. Evidently he was a believer in the old Arab proverb that "a well populated head is a sign of a generous mind."

King Hussein was particularly fond of mules and had one of the finest mule stables in the world. He had brought them from South America, Australia, Abyssinia, and even from Missouri. It was a common sight to see him galloping out of Mecca on the way to his suburban palace mounted on the back of his favorite white mule.

Hussein was a firm believer in prohibition. He hated alcohol, and if he found any one intoxicated on the streets of Mecca he punished him unmercifully. On one occasion two of Lawrence's Arab warriors celebrated a victorious engagement with the Turks by going to Mecca for a holiday. They took along a few bottles of *arak*. News of their escapades reached the ears of the king, and he had them flogged in the public square. Hussein also disliked talking-machines. He said that they were the invention of the devil, and not the invention of Thomas A. Edison. He would not allow them to be brought to his capital.

On one occasion while resting under a palm-tree with his retinue he saw an Arab sneak a head-cloth from his neighbor and hide it under his skirt. When the owner began searching for it, all denied having seen it. Then the king leaped to his feet, walked over to the guilty Arab, and gave him a terrific blow in the ribs with his gnarled club. The thief never recovered.

But King Hussein no longer rules in Mecca. Not long after the end of the World War one of his blood-enemies, Sultan Ibn Sa'ud, swept out of the Central Arabian Desert and made himself king of the Hedjaz. Two of Hussein's sons, however, still rule over Near Eastern countries, Abdullah on the throne of Transjordania, and Feisal in Mesopotamia.

To live in the desert you must be quick-witted. Death is always lurking just over the next sand-dune. Fortunately Lawrence was as keen mentally as any Arab. Frequently his life was saved by quick thinking. On one occasion when he was riding south across the desert with a half-breed Haurani who was a famous camel rider, they suddenly came upon a dozen Arabs. Strangers were galloping over the sand-dunes to cut them off. They shouted for Lawrence and Dhami to dismount and at the same time did so themselves. But Lawrence recognized them as members of the Beni-Sakr tribe, enemies of the followers of Hussein and Feisal. So of course Lawrence and Dhami remained in their camel saddles. While the Beni-Sakr shouted friendly greetings they also had their fingers on their triggers. Lawrence knew that he was in a tight corner. Suddenly he amazed the Beni-

Sakr by smiling cordially and saying to the leader of the band:

"Come near; I want to whisper something to you." Swinging half out of his saddle he asked the Beni-Sakr sheik:

"Do you know what your name is?"

The brigand looked rather dumfounded, and then Lawrence added:

"I think it must be 'Terrace'!"

This word has a special Arab meaning and is the most terrible insult that can be offered to any one in the desert. The Beni-Sakr sheik was momentarily speechless, unable to understand how any traveler who was so outnumbered would dare say such a thing. Before the sheik could regain his wits Lawrence shouted to the crowd of Beni-Sakr:

"May Allah give you peace!"

Then he and the Haurani swung their camels into a gallop and disappeared over the nearest sand-dune. A moment later the Beni-Sakr were after them, firing wildly, but Lawrence and Dhami were soon out of range.

The Arab women played a very small part in the campaign. The wives and daughters of the Bedouin sheiks remained at home in the black tents. Instead of speaking of her as his wife the Bedouin uses the phrase, "the relative in my house," or, "the mother of my son Abdullah."

The women of the desert and the women of the villages and towns are very different. Those who lead a nomadic life are thin and lean like their wiry husbands and sons. Their city cousins are usually very fat and spend nearly all their time indoors. The Bedouin woman does not keep her face covered. But the Arab woman who lives in a settled community never goes into the street unveiled. All female slaves captured in war become the private property of the man who wins them. Although Arabia is a land of romance, it is not exactly a paradise for the gentler sex.

CHAPTER XX

LAWRENCE WIPES OUT A TURKISH REGIMENT

ONE more battle took place before Lawrence started his great march north, the march that was to end with the spectacular capture of Damascus and the downfall of the Turkish Empire. This isolated engagement occurred on a low ridge of hills and in a valley just a little more than a hundred miles to the north and east of Akaba. A Turkish regiment under a general named Hamid Fakhri Bey had been sent down from Syria to attempt to retake some of the territory that Lawrence and his Arabs had occupied. Fakhri had cavalry, mountain artillery, and German machine-gun squads in addition to his infantry.

The Turks first came to grips with the

Arab outposts in the valley of Seil El Hasa near the town of Tafilek, a few miles east of the Damascus-Medina railway line. The Turks were victorious at the start and drove the Arabs into the town. Emir Feisal's young brother, Prince Zeid, was in command, but Lawrence was there as the guiding spirit.

The terror-stricken villagers were dumping their household effects out of their homes, and Bedouins were galloping up and down the streets engaged in their favorite occupation of wasting ammunition by blazing it off into the dark. So long as Lawrence and the British were supplying them with bullets, every night was like a Fourth of July celebration for them.

At dawn the Turks opened fire with their artillery. Lawrence did what he could to mass his regular fighting men for a pitched battle. He ran from one group to another arousing them to a frenzy. With a great shout the Arabs charged and drove the Turks over the first ridge of hills on to a small plain. Casualties were heavy on both sides. The Turks were firing fairly accurately, and steel fragments from their bursting shells glanced from the rocks and played havoc among Lawrence's men. But Prince Zeid now came rushing up with a mountain-gun and all of the machine-guns that his forces possessed.

The Turks suddenly decided to slip around both sides of the ridge of hills and thus cut off the Arabs from any possible retreat. At this moment a squadron of German aëroplanes came diving out of the sky, dropping bombs and training their machine-guns on the scattered Arabs. Noon came and still the firing continued without much advantage to either side. But Lawrence had sent off couriers to try to round up other straggling Bedouin bands who were known to be a few miles away. Reserves began to pour in between two and three o'clock. The Turks were gaining ground now and forcing Lawrence and his men to drop back from the ridge of hills.

But as they retreated Lawrence coolly counted the number of paces he ran so that he could give his artillery the exact distance from their new position to the top of the ridge which the Turks had now seized.

A little later he opened fire with his mountain-gun, and nearly every shell tore holes in the Turkish ranks. Once more Lawrence and the chief Bedouin sheiks shouted for a charge. The newly arrived Bedouin cavalry were on hand to help them now. With their banners waving in the air they swept up the hill, right through the Turkish ranks. Just at sunset the Turks gave up the fight, and the entire regiment with all its guns and horses fell into the hands of the victorious desert warriors. It was a brilliant victory for Lawrence and was largely due to the cool way in which he had handled the straggling crowd of undisciplined men who were with him on that day. The battlefield at Seil El Hasa was strewn with dead and wounded. Among the killed was the Turkish general Hamid Fakhri Bey.

Many picturesque desert sheiks were associated with Lawrence now, and more were pouring in from all corners of the desert. The news of the many victories spread rapidly over the sand-dunes to every oasis. Among these picturesque "drinkers of the milk of war" was a nephew of old Auda Abu Tayi, the Bedouin Robin Hood. This fiery youngster was Zaal Ibn Motlog, the Beau Brummel of the Howeitat. With his carefully curled mustache, his sharp pointed beard, and his resplendent robes and headdress he made a striking picture.

Another who had brought in four thousand fighting warriors was Motlog Ibn Jemiaan, whose chief delight was to go along with Lawrence on train-wrecking expeditions. Until he joined Lawrence he had never seen an automobile. The Arab forces now had a number of cars in addition to the Rolls-Royce armored squadron. Some of these were little Ford trucks. One day two of Lawrence's fellow-officers were starting out on a short trip by car, and they invited Motlog Ibn Jemiaan to clamber aboard and ride along with them. The Ford careened back and forth wildly, and in rounding a turn poor Motlog Ibn Jemiaan was dumped off into the sand, landing head first. When the officers stopped the car and ran back to help brush him off and apologize for the accident, the old sheik shook his head sadly and said:

"Please don't be angry with me. You see I haven't learned how to ride these strange things yet."

The sheik had an idea that learning to ride in a motor-car was something that had to come through long experience, like riding a racing camel.

CHAPTER XXI

FOOLING THE TURKS WITH A FAKE ARMY

FROM now on Lawrence's forces became the right wing of Allenby's army. The British crusaders fighting in Palestine had freed the southern half of the Holy Land, and their front line stretched across from the Mediterranean Sea coast to Jerusalem, Jericho, and on into the little known Arabian Desert, where Lawrence and his wild followers were raiding.

Although Jerusalem had been captured, the sacred city of Nazareth, the hills around the Sea of Galilee, and the whole of Syria still remained in the hands of the Turks. So the war with the Turks was a long way from completion.

There were two ways of winning the final victory. One was to fight the Turks back, mile by mile; the other, to try a bold stroke and clear them out at once. Allenby decided to take the big chance. He made his daring decision partly because he knew he could depend on young Colonel Lawrence to give him timely help.

It was now that the Germans in France were making their last big drive. Things were going badly for the Allies, and Ludendorff was about to make his final smash toward Paris. The Allies were so hard pressed and in such desperate straits that they simply had to call on Allenby to send nearly all of the flower of his fine army to France—excepting his dashing Australian and New Zealand cavalry and a few infantry regiments. This he did, but it was a bitter blow and left him with a mere skeleton of an army.

How now could he hope to make his big attack? There was only one way. He must somehow create a new army. But where were the men to come from? He decided to try using Indian divisions from Mesopotamia and various other odd bodies of soldiers—anything he could get, even raw recruits who knew nothing of war.

He had intended to strike his big blow in June or July of 1918, and with Lawrence he had talked this all over and made a combined plan. But now it seemed as if he could not get anything like a good fighting force together before October. Very well, he would have to wait until October. Not at all what he had hoped for, but it was the best way out of a bad hole.

Lawrence was called over to Palestine again, and his advice was that the delay would be a bad thing. The success of the big smash would depend on his Arabs to no small extent, and in October he would not have any of his best desert fighters left. Autumn was the time when the Bedouins moved with their tents and flocks to the winter grazing grounds on the plateaus of Central Arabia. His nervous tribesmen, who were impatient at best, would begin to think about the green oases in Central Arabia.

They would go wandering away with their camels, sheep, and tents whether they were needed or not. These freedom-loving people could not be held like ordinary troops.

"Besides," said he, "the autumn rains in the Holy Land are always heavy, and if you do not strike before they come, then your soldiers, cannon, and supplies will be stuck in the mud half the time."

Allenby agreed, changed his plan, and ordered the great drive for September. He knew he would never in the world be able to get his miscellaneous groups of raw soldiers trained well enough by then. He also knew he could not depend on plain fighting. So he would have to make up for the weakness and inexperience of his troops by depending considerably on Lawrence, and working some trick on the enemy. What kind of trick? Well, it was to be something like the feint a boxer makes when he shoots out with one hand, as if he were going to hit you with it, and then quick as a flash hauls off and hits you with the other.

On the right of Allenby's line, over toward the desert, was the river Jordan, which runs into the Dead Sea. It lies in a famous valley, the one where John the Baptist baptized Christ. Up a valley is the usual way for an army to advance. Generally speaking, you do not march along the hilltops, but you follow the valleys. The Turks would expect the British to make their main push up the Jordan. So Allenby decided to trick them into thinking that such was exactly what he meant to do.

He gave them a kind of imitation motion-picture of an army getting ready for a big drive up the Jordan, and shifted all his camel hospitals to the Jordan Valley. In Egypt were hundreds of worn-out tents, which he had sent up and pitched along the banks of the sacred river. Ten thousand horse-blankets were thrown over bushes in the valley and tied up to look like lines of horses, and five new bridges of boats, pontoon bridges, were thrown across the river. He arranged every sort of fake thing that

LAWRENCE'S TULIPS

his officers could think of; consequently when the Turkish and German planes flew over the enemy, airmen would look down and rush back to headquarters with the news that a big army, ready to fight its way up the valley of the Jordan, had assembled north of Jericho. All the Turkish cannon that had been captured were hauled over there, and Allenby began blazing them away at the Turks encamped in the Hills of Moab. All in all it was the biggest hoax put over since the Greeks captured Troy with the aid of the famous Wooden Horse.

Lawrence, of course, had an important share in preparing this gigantic camouflage. He sent some of his most prominent sheiks to the country around Damascus with seven thousand pounds in gold (about thirty-five thousand dollars), to buy barley. The sheiks bought barley recklessly in every town and village they came to. The Turks knew that Lawrence's Bedouin cavalry could not use up such vast quantities of grain, and hence they supposed it surely must be intended for large forces of Allenby's cavalry—that army in the valley of the Jordan!

Then Lawrence set out to attack the Turkish garrison at Mudawara, on the Damascus-Medina railway, not far from the Dead Sea and Jordan. There was a lively fight for twenty minutes—nothing particularly savage, just a feint to make the Turks think the big attack was coming in that territory. Colonel Robin Buxton and his camel corps from Palestine came over to handle the affair, and did it nobly. Lawrence himself led his Arabs against Amman, just east of the Jordan—another feint.

In a short time the Turks were sure the Jordan Valley must be swarming with Allenby's soldiers. Turkish aëroplanes flew over constantly on scouting trips, and the more they saw of the fake camp and the fake horses the more badly they were fooled. As a matter of fact Allenby had very few soldiers around the Jordan. There were three battalions, two of which were Jewish soldiers from England and the United

States, for he was concentrating the rest of his men and guns for his big surprise drive a long distance away from the Jordan. If the Turks had guessed the truth they could have rushed straight down the Jordan Valley, pushed behind Allenby's line, and recaptured Jerusalem. But they never suspected. They were outguessed.

Lawrence now spread the rumor that he and his Arabs were going to attack Deraa, an important railway junction just south of Damascus. A push against this town would seem like a part of the fake attack up the Jordan. As a matter of fact, he really did intend to take Deraa. The cutting of the railroad there would put the Turks in something of a bad way when the real attack was made on the other side of the line. Why did Lawrence spread the news of what he really intended to do? It was a kind of double deception The Turks would believe that any report so generally spread about, which everybody had heard, had been sent out to fool them. They would surmise that

Deraa was just the place that Lawrence did *not* intend to attack. Then Lawrence, pretending the greatest secrecy, told a few chosen people that he was going to make a raid against Amman, a town some distance from Deraa. He knew that some of the people to whom he gave this very confidential information would babble. They did. First the Turks got the general loud rumor that Deraa would be attacked and then the confidential news that it was not Deraa but Amman. You can guess which of the two reports they believed. They prepared to defend Amman.

Lawrence's plan was to swing far out across the unmapped desert, away around the eastern end of the Turkish line, and cut around against Deraa from the rear. In the course of this maneuver a curious fight took place. Have you ever heard of horsemen sinking a fleet? Well, that was what happened.

CHAPTER XXII

LAWRENCE BAITS THE BIG TRAP

AT a town on the Dead Sea, not far from the ancient cities of Sodom and Gomorrah, the Turks had a naval base. It was the headquarters of their Dead Sea fleet. The fleet consisted of a few ancient tubs and several motor-driven craft armed with light guns. These *battle-ships* were moored near shore. The officers were having breakfast in a Turkish mess near-by, and had no idea enemies were around. But a small squad of Lawrence's Arabs, led by Abu Irgeig, came along slyly, to take a look at the navy. They saw at a glance the decks of the boats were deserted, save for a few sentries, and so the Arabs got off their horses, made a sudden rush, and clambered aboard the boats like Barbary pirates. They scuppered the crews and scuttled the boats, then got back to their horses and were away across the desert before the amazed Turkish officers knew what it was all about. The Turkish Dead Sea fleet was sunk.

Lawrence's little army having got near Deraa, the next step was to cut the railroad to keep reinforcements from being sent up. The young Englishman used the armored cars he had with him. One fine day these war autos whizzed down the railroad track and captured a Turkish post before the astonished defenders were aware their enemies were near. Close at hand was a fine bridge which had been built by Abdul Hamid, the Red Sultan. Lawrence scampered out along the trestle and placed three tulips, each containing a hundred and fifty pounds of gun-cotton, one at either end of the bridge and one at the middle. He touched them off, and with a great boom the bridge crashed down. Back to the armored cars he and his men dashed, and then away for more adventure. Five miles north they surprised another railroad post and captured the Turkish soldiers. An enemy cavalry detachment of wild-eyed Kurds from the hills near Persia came up, and rifles and machine-guns rattled while the Kurdish horsemen were wiped out. Lawrence then blew up another bridge, ripped up six hundred pairs of rails, thereby thoroughly crippling the railroad line, and called it a day.

The little Arab army took a position on the top of a high promontory from which it could clearly see Deraa four miles away. Through his field-glasses Lawrence could pick out nine enemy aëroplanes on the flying field. The presence of the attacking force, was now known, and the German aviators proceeded to make things hot for them. They circled overhead, dived and swooped, and dropped bombs, at the same time raking the Arabs with their machine-guns. The Bedouins tried to fire back at the war-birds with rifles and light cannon, but that had little effect. However, Lawrence had more with him than horses, camels, and a few armored cars; he had one antiquated old aëroplane, piloted by Captain Junor. With bombs and machine-guns, the German air squadron was busy at it overhead when Junor in his ancient bus sailed right into the middle of them. The German machines were more than a match for him, and the men on the ground anxiously watched the air fight over the Arabian Desert.

There were eight enemy planes, four two-seaters and four scout machines. Junor cruised right through them and kept going, the enemy planes turning after him as he led the whole circus westward. They all disappeared and Lawrence and his men wondered sadly what would become of poor Junor and his ramshackle bus. But twenty minutes later Junor came tearing back with the enemy still at his heels and shooting at him. He signaled to Lawrence that he was out of gas and would have to land, and came down safely within fifty yards of the Arabs. The old plane turned over on its back, gave a chug, and "passed out." A German machine swooped down at it, and let go a bomb. A direct hit! Lawrence saw his one aëroplane go up in a cloud of sand and kindling wood, but luckily the pilot had jumped out of his seat and rushed away a few moments before. The only part of his machine that was not destroyed was the Lewis machine-gun. Within half an hour Junor had transferred it to a Ford truck and was tearing around outside of Deraa and shooting at the Turks with tracer bullets, the kind that leave trails of smoke behind so that the airman can see where his shots are going.

The air battle was scarcely over when Lawrence was on his way to join a detachment he had sent to cut the main telegraph line between Palestine and Syria. This was tremendously important. If the attempt succeeded, it would break the one line of communication between the Turkish armies and their base. It succeeded all right. Charges of gun-cotton were planted, and telegraph poles were blown up one after another.

Many of the Arabs of the surrounding country joined the detachment, and on the following day Lawrence marched along the railroad toward Palestine right in the heart of the enemy country. He spent most of that day planting tulips, and near Nasib he blew up his seventy-ninth bridge, a rather large one with three fine arches. Knowing that the final victory was probably close at hand, and that this might be his last bridge, he planted twice as many tulips as necessary. That made a fine bang, and he thoroughly enjoyed it, for he was not too much of a scholar to get plenty of amusement out of a sight like that.

Next day he was joined by his armored cars, and, keeping along the railroad, came in sight of an enemy flying field. With two armored cars he sped across the open country to take a closer look. If it had not been for a deep gully in front of them, the cars would have rushed the planes. As it was, they could only fire on the war-birds with machine-guns. With fifteen hundred bullets they disabled one on the ground, but the other two took off and came swooping over them. The Germans circled around like great birds, pouring streams of lead down at the armored cars. The cars dashed away. The planes went after them, and darted down at them, dropping bombs. Nobody was hurt except Colonel Lawrence, who was wounded in the hand by shrapnel. Lawrence said that after horse and camel back, he considered this armored car work as "fighting de luxe."

One of Lawrence's Arab lieutenants who distinguished himself during these adventures was Jaafar Pasha, the man who had once been a general in the Turkish army and who now was the commander-in-chief of Emir Feisal's regulars, the force that Colonel Joyce had built up.

A former Turkish officer who was Lawrence's comrade in arms during those days was Jaafar's brother-in-law, Nuri Said. He had attended Turkish Staff College. In the Balkan War, when the Turks fought against the Christians to the north of them, he served as an aviator.

Even in those days, long before the World War, the Arabs were trying to find a way to get free from the Turks, and Nuri had joined a secret society of Arab officers in the Turkish army who were plotting to overthrow Turkish rule in their country. It is quite natural that when Lawrence stirred up the revolt in the desert Nuri was not long in joining King Hussein and Emir Feisal.

Lawrence's army of Arabs was lurking around Deraa, trying to take the city; the Turks and their German officers were greatly alarmed, for the city was so important as the center of railway communication, with yards and locomotives and cars and big stores of supplies, that they simply had to hold it. And, besides, they thought that Lawrence's army of desert tribesmen was beginning what was to be Allenby's big push up the Jordan Valley. They concentrated the main body of their soldiers in that region, to hold Deraa and block the supposed advance. This left the other parts of their line weakly held. Allenby's real advance was at the extreme opposite end of the line.

Instead of sending his right wing up the Jordan, all of his attacking forces were concentrated on his left wing, away over by the Mediterranean Sea. When the big smash came, the British went over the top along the section near the seaport of Jaffa. They easily broke through the thin screen of Turks, and, once they were through, there were no enemy forces in the rear of the line to stop them. The Turks, completely deceived, were massed away over on the other side of Palestine, waiting for an attack that never came; an attack which really amounted to nothing more than old junk tents and horse-blankets tied to bushes. Hundreds of Turks were killed and many more captured, and the survivors turned into a mob of running men, whom the British aviators, swooping after them, kept on the run.

CHAPTER XXIII

THE TURKS SMASHED AND DAMASCUS TAKEN

SO swift and unexpected was the advance that Allenby's men were in important towns far back of the line before the Turkish commanders ever dreamed of it. When the important railway junction at Afuleh was captured with its huge depots of stores, the Turkish motor-trucks kept rumbling on and into the town, never knowing that it was in the hands of the British. They came in a steady stream, drawing up to the supply station, while a British officer at the station stood and directed them as if he were some very polite German traffic cop.

"This way, please," he called to the drivers, one after another, and the trucks pulled over to the places where he directed them;

only then did they learn they had run straight into the enemy's hands. This continued for four hours, until the astonishing word spread among the Turks in the country to the rear that the British were at the railroad junction.

Six hours after Allenby's men were in Afuleh, a German aëroplane came flying over and landed. Two men got out and walked over to headquarters to report. They were bringing orders from Hindenburg to Liman von Sanders, the German commander of the Turks. It was only when they saw British uniforms at headquarters that they guessed what had happened, and they became a couple of angry Germans when they had to deliver Hindenburg's message, not to Liman von Sanders, but to a British officer who forwarded it to Allenby.

During this time Lawrence and his Arabs were still in front of Deraa. The young English scholar was raiding far and wide, blowing up sections of railroad. It was hard for the Turks to move their soldiers while

Allenby's column was swooping along on the other side of the line. Lawrence's job now was to keep the Turks busy in his section, and to do what he could to stop their retreat when Allenby came swinging up. It was to be something like bringing the end of a noose around to close a trap.

One of Lawrence's companions in these final days was a Lord Winterton, a belted earl and quite an adventurous fighter. One night the earl had a peculiar experience. He was in command of a party destroying a section of railroad, and his men were planting tulips along the line. Winterton was walking along when a soldier came up and asked:

"How are things going?"

"Fine," replied Winterton. "We have twenty-eight tulips planted, and will be ready to touch them off in a few minutes."

"Splendid," said the soldier, and disappeared.

A few minutes later machine-guns blazed on all sides, and the earl and his men had

LAWRENCE'S SQUADRON OF ARMORED ROLLS-ROYCES

to run for it. The soldier he had spoken to was either a German or a Turk who knew English perfectly. He had happened to stray upon the railroad wrecking party, had seen what was going on, and had acted his part as coolly as an actor on the stage, hurrying to bring up a Turkish detachment stationed near-by.

The earl's show was a success, though. He had time, before he cleared out, to set the tulips off, and the railroad bed blew up.

The Turks had nine aëroplanes near Deraa, and they were playing the very dickens with the young archæologist's Arabs, for day after day they sailed out and dropped bombs on the Bedouins. Lawrence got a plane and flew over to Allenby, asking him to send several fighting planes to drive off the German machines, so Allenby gave him three Bristol fighters, the best battleplanes the British had in the Holy Land. One of the pilots was a Captain Ross Smith, who later was to become famous for being the first man to fly from England to Australia. The Bristol fighters were better machines than those the Turks had, and they soon put a stop to the German habit of bombing the Arabs.

One morning, while Lawrence and his aviators were having breakfast together, a Turkish plane came flying over. One of the airmen immediately jumped into his plane and took off from the level field of sand. Up he went after the enemy, and the Turkish plane tried to get away; but the Bristol fighter, which was much faster, caught up and pumped machine-gun bullets in a steady stream till the enemy scout fell in flames. The English aviator then returned and finished his porridge, which had been kept hot for him. He had begun to eat his marmalade when another enemy war-bird appeared. The British pilot went up after him, but this time the Turk was too cunning and made away at once. By now a second British machine, piloted by Captain Ross Smith, had taken off and was in the chase. He succeeded in catching the enemy plane and sent it down in flames. That night the Germans burned their remaining aircraft, and the British controlled the sky.

Soon afterward Allenby sent a big Handley-Page bombing plane to help Lawrence. It was really meant more to impress the Arabs than to damage the Turks. The Bedouins had never seen such a big fighting swallow, as they called it. It made such an impression on them that many of the neighboring tribesmen who had hitherto refused to join Lawrence's force now came in.

Jaafar, he of the large waist and jovial smile, led a force of his men down the line to have a look at the first big bridge that had been blown up by Lawrence. They found that the Turks were repairing it and nearly had it in good shape again. There was a lively fight. The Turkish soldiers doing the work were guarded by a company of German machine-gunners. These were game fighters and gave Jaafar's men a tough argument, but finally the Arabs drove them away and burned the great timber framework the Germans and Turks had put up.

The Turks in Deraa still held the town, and Lawrence decided to drive them out of it by throwing his force of Arabs across the line between Deraa and Damascus. That was the way by which the Turks would have to retreat, for seeing they were in danger of being surrounded, they would have to clear out as fast as they could. At the head of his camel corps he made a swift march and swept down on the railroad between Deraa and Damascus. This was a point where he had blown up the line on one of his previous raids, but the Turks worked furiously and had repaired it. The railroad had been opened for trains just the previous day, and Lawrence now planted a huge crop of tulips, blowing up ties and tracks once more, and making a thorough job of it. Six complete trains were pent up in Deraa. The Turks, feeling that their line of retreat was threatened by the camel corps, immediately marched out of Deraa to fight their way through, while Lawrence and his Arabs were scouting the country and picking up what Turks they could. They captured two Austro-Turk machine-gun companies. Lawrence climbed to the summit of a large hill, from which he could sweep the country with his glasses. Whenever he saw a small force of Turks appear on the horizon, he jumped on his horse and at the head of nine hundred of his best desert fighters swooped down on the enemy. But if, as he watched from the hill, he saw that the force of Turks was too large for him to tackle, he let it pass.

An aëroplane dropped him a message saying it had sighted two columns of Turks. One, six thousand strong, was coming from Deraa—it was the force that was retreating from that town—the other was of two thousand men approaching from another direction. Lawrence decided the smaller was about his size. He sent an order for his forces of Arab foot-soldiers to hurry up, and had his horsemen hang around the flanks of the Turkish column to annoy it. Soon a big battle was raging. The two armies lay opposite each other, advancing, retreating, and firing always. The Arab horsemen swarmed around the Turks, picking off men when they could.

In the course of the long battle the Turks retired from the village of Tafas, and Lawrence and his officers rode through it. At Lawrence's side was Tallal, one of the strongest fighting men of Arabia. He had been one of the leaders of the Arab revolt, one of Lawrence's stanchest supporters. He was the sheik of the village of Tafas, which the advancing Arabs now had entered. The town was a scene of horror. Before retiring, the Turks had massacred the people, women, children, and all. Tallal, the sheik, saw pools of blood and in them lying the wives and children of his tribesmen.

"The best of you brings me the most Turkish dead," said Lawrence.

Tallal groaned as if he had been wounded. Then he rode on to a hill and sat there on his mare staring at the line of Turks ahead.

Presently he wrapped his head-cloth about his face, spurred his horse, and rode down the slope toward the Turkish line. On he went, one man against the enemy. The Arabs stopped shooting, and the Turks stopped shooting too, as if in astonishment. He was only a few lengths from the enemy when he stood up in his saddle and twice cried his war-cry, then dashed on. Rifles and machine-guns crashed out in the lines of the Turks, and Tallal and his mare fell riddled with bullets.

Wild with rage the Arabs swooped down on the Turks. There was no staying them. The slaughter of their women and children had turned them blood mad. The Turks broke and ran. The Arabs gave no quarter but killed every man they came upon. Two German machine-gun companies were grouped around three motor-cars that carried high officers. In one car was Djemal Pasha, the Turkish commander-in-chief. The Arabs attacked them with a crazy rage, but the German machine-gunners resisted magnificently and drove their assailants off with fierce bursts of fire. Still fighting, they made their way from the field and escaped.

That day Lawrence's Arabs entered Deraa.

The whole force of Turks was now in flight before Allenby's advancing columns. The regiments that had gone through at Jaffa, on the Mediterranean, continued their rapid advance and threatened to round up the enemy's armies. Lawrence and his Arabs were along the line of the retreating fugitives. They were too weak a force to dam the retreat completely and, as a matter of fact, were in danger of being swamped by the fleeing horde. They kept striking, though, falling upon every detachment not too large for their strength, cutting off supplies and harassing the retreat in every way. Lawrence led his force to the outskirts of Damascus. The city was a sea of flame. The Turks were fleeing, burning their stores and blowing up their ammunition dumps.

At sunset Lawrence, in the Rolls-Royce that had served him so well in his fighting, drove into Damascus. Allenby's troops had not yet come up, and the twenty-nine-year-old scholar who was the commander-in-chief of the greatest army that had been raised in Arabia for five hundred years was master of the ancient Arabian capital. The entire population lined the streets to look at the slight blond young man dressed in the garb of a prince of Mecca. Knowing they were at last freed from the Turkish yoke, they shouted his name and Emir Feisal's in a joyous chorus. For ten miles along the streets of the oldest city in the world, the crowds gave the boyish-looking Englishman one of the greatest ovations any man has ever received. For four days Lawrence was the ruler of Damascus. He visited the tomb of Saladin, the Moslem conqueror of earlier times. The kaiser had visited the shrine in 1898, and had placed in it a satin flag and a bronze wreath on which was inscribed in Turkish and Arabic:

From one great emperor to another.

This rather bombastic memento had irritated Lawrence on his pre-war visits to Damascus. The bronze wreath is now in the office of the curator of the British War Museum. The flag went home with me.

CHAPTER XXIV

ABD EL KEDER, THE TREACHEROUS EMIR

AFTER the fall of Damascus the combined British and Arab forces drove the Turks from the Syrian seaport of Beirut, from Baalbek, Homs, and Hamah, and then swept on north to the great city of Aleppo, long the capital of Saladin, the Saracen. When Allenby and Lawrence's armored cars, galloping horsemen, and racing camel riders swept through the gates in the massive wall around Aleppo and occupied Saladin's lofty citadel, the war in the East was over. The Turks were overwhelmed. They threw down their arms. If they had not done so Allenby and Lawrence's irresistible cavalry would have swept them into the Golden Horn.

With the fall of Aleppo the onrushing armies of Allenby and Lawrence had thrown themselves across the Near Eastern railway lines which converge at that city. Most important of all, they now were astride the far-famed Berlin-to-Bagdad railroad, the line by which Kaiser Wilhelm had hoped to build up a vast Mitteleuropa empire stretching from the North Sea to the Persian Gulf.

With the fall of Aleppo, Allenby and Lawrence had not only smashed the old Ottoman Empire but had liberated four important Asiatic countries from the Turkish yoke: Arabia, Palestine, Syria, and Mesopotamia. During the last six weeks of this great cavalry campaign, Allenby's and Lawrence's horsemen and armored cars advanced through the Turkish lines and fought their way deep into Turkish territory for a distance of about six hundred miles. They captured a hundred thousand Turks and two hundred big guns, destroyed scores of aëroplanes, seized vast supply-dumps and strings of motor-trucks, and annihilated several Turkish armies.

I believe that historians of the future will agree that this final drive in the romantic lands of the Near East was the most successful cavalry movement of all time. The credit for the brilliant strategy will mostly go to Field-Marshal Viscount Allenby, the giant British general who succeeded where Richard the Lion-Hearted had failed, and to the undersized, five-foot-three youth, Ned Lawrence, who led the desert warriors.

Turkey had surrendered. Far to the north, in Europe, Germany was nearing her final hour. In Arabia only one small further fighting point demanded attention. You will remember that the Holy City of Medina, the birthplace of the Prophet, had long been held by a stubborn Turkish army under the command of that fire-eater, Fakhri Pasha. In the midst of the desert, surrounded by enemy tribes, this lone Turkish tiger held out.

The end of the war and the signing of a Turkish-Allied Armistice meant nothing to Fakhri Pasha, who was a "fighting fool" if there ever was one. He swore that he would never surrender to the Arabs, and that was all there was to it. After the collapse of Turkey came the downfall of the Austrians, Bulgars, and Germans. The world now busied itself with peace treaties. But in far-off Arabia, around Medina, the war was still on.

Fakhri Pasha knew well that no help could ever come to him. Of the twenty thousand men who had made up his army in the beginning, eleven thousand remained. The Arabs were still harassing them, and their food supplies were cut off. The British offered to protect the stern old Turk and his troops from the Arabs, if they would surrender. They would be treated well, and could return to their homes as they liked. But Fakhri Pasha declared that rather than turn over his sword he would blow up the holy places of Medina, and himself and his soldiers along with them.

His food supplies were exhausted. For days and weeks his garrison had nothing to eat except their last horses and camels and the dates that grew just outside the city wall. Fakhri Pasha never did surrender. But his soldiers, despite their love and admiration for their plucky commander, grew weary of their hardships and their hopeless position. It was all very well for Fakhri to declare that he would blow up the city and garrison, but for their part these Turkish soldiers wanted to get home to their wives and children. So they seized the old tiger and virtually held him a prisoner until they could surrender the city.

A couple of years later, while traveling in Central Asia, I ran across the gallant Fakhri. He was the ambassador for the new Turkish government at the court of Amanullah Khan, ruler of Afghanistan. The grizzled old hero had lost none of his fire. He was working for his country as bravely as ever, this time at the arts of diplomacy rather than those of war.

But to return to Colonel Lawrence: although peace had come, he was still having exciting times. During his short rule in Damascus trouble broke out in the city. There was a prominent Arab from North Africa who was a bitter enemy of Feisal. Emir Abd El Keder hailed from Algiers, now a colony of France. His grandfather, who was also named Abd El Keder, had fought against the French for many years, and finally had been forced to flee to Damascus. When the World War came, the younger Abd El Keder and a brother joined the Turks. The two grandsons of the old rebel made as much trouble for the Allies as they could. The brother served as an agent for the Turks and Germans in Africa, where he tried to induce the Mohammedans of the Sahara Desert to invade Egypt. Abd El Keder played a wicked, treacherous part in the war in the Arabian Desert.

He pretended to join the cause of Arab independence. He arranged with the Turks to stage a mock escape from Constantinople, and fled to Feisal's base-camp at Akaba. He talked so eloquently about his devotion to the cause of Arab patriotism that Feisal welcomed him, received him into his army, and gave him an honorary title. While Abd El Keder seemed to serve Emir Feisal with enthusiastic devotion, he was in fact nothing more than a super-spy for the Turks. He sent the Turkish leaders reports of what was going on among the Arabs, and waited for a good opportunity to betray Feisal's armies.

His chance came when Lawrence set out to destroy an important bridge in the rear of the Turkish army. Abd El Keder begged to be allowed to go along. He had wide lands in the neighborhood of the bridge, and it really seemed as though his help would be useful. So Lawrence took him and a force of his men along. The party rode north across the desert for many days, until they drew near the bridge. Then, at night, Abd El Keder and his followers stole away, joined the Turks, and revealed Lawrence's plan. He pointed out how the young Englishman and the small force he had left could easily be wiped out. Lawrence soon realized that he was betrayed. He had only a few men remaining with him, and he knew that the traitor would quickly bring the enemy swooping down on him. Still he determined to try to blow up the bridge. He had a narrow escape. The Turks, directed by the traitor, came up before he had time to set off his tulips, and he and his handful of men had to scurry away across the desert for their lives.

The Turks showered Abd El Keder with honors. Later on, when Allenby made his last great drive on Damascus, with Lawrence and his Arabs sweeping around on the right wing, the Turkish officials sent their Algerian spy out among the villagers in the rear of their retreating army to prevent an uprising. Abd El Keder went, but when he saw that the Turks were thoroughly beaten, he deserted the losing side as rats desert a sinking ship. He began to talk Arab patriotism again, hurried to Damascus, and arrived there a few hours before Lawrence and his Bedouins rode in. The Turks had left, and the city had no government. Abd El Keder had a few hours in which to get in his cunning work. He quickly organized a nationalist government for the city, with himself at the head, and made preparations to give the advancing British army a triumphal reception. He would receive the victors as the leader of the Damascus civil administration. He thought he could easily impose on Allenby and the British officers and work himself into a position of power. Imagine his surprise and disappointment when he had to deal, not with Allenby and the British command, but with Colonel Lawrence, who occupied the city at the head of his Arabs. It was awkward for him to have to do business with the man he had betrayed and who knew him through and through. As a matter of fact, he did not have a chance to do any business at all. Lawrence immediately ordered the treacherous emir and his men to resign, and appointed loyal followers of Feisal in their stead. Abd El Keder tried to argue, but he and his henchmen were treated with little ceremony. They were so enraged that they drew their weapons and would have attacked Lawrence, had not the others present seized and disarmed them. Among these was old Auda Abu Tayi.

Abd El Keder and his brother, who had joined him, now tried to make all the trouble they could for Lawrence and his government. With other malcontents like themselves, they went among the people of the city and preached rebellion against Feisal. Rioting broke out. There was fighting in the street. The trouble was only quelled when Lawrence's Arabs met a mob of Abd El Keder's followers in the central square of Damascus and turned machine-guns on them. Many were killed and wounded, and the others scurried away.

The rebellion was put down, and the two trouble-making Algerian brothers went into hiding. They kept under cover for a while, planning a new outbreak. But Abd El Keder became so angry one day that it cost him his life. He galloped down to Feisal's palace waving his rifle, and shouted for Feisal to come out and fight with him. Then he began shooting. One of the soldiers on guard at the palace fired back and sent a bullet through his head. After that the trouble ceased.

CHAPTER XXV

LAWRENCE STILL A MAN OF MYSTERY

HAVING helped his Arab friends in waging war, Lawrence now helped in making peace. The Allied governments, in encouraging the Arabs to continue their revolt and even carry their war out of Arabia and into Syria, had promised the Arabs complete independence. But these promises conflicted with the real desires of some of the Allied nations. France wanted Syria as a part of her colonial empire. The Jews wanted Palestine in spite of the fact that its population was almost wholly Arab. The Italians and Greeks both looked with longing eyes toward the Near East. The British were anxious to hold the Sinai Peninsula as a means of protecting the Suez Canal.

So it was evident to Lawrence that the Arab war was only half won. They had won on the battle-fields of the Near East, but now they must go and fight the battle of the peace conference in Paris. With the end of the World War and the downfall of Germany and Turkey, Lawrence felt that he had done all he could for his own country. So when he went to Paris with the Arab delegates he went in order to help them merely hold what they already had won in battle.

Emir Feisal, Lawrence's "veiled prophet," was there as the chief Arab peace representative. The Arabian emir and his picturesque staff in their Oriental robes made a striking impression in Paris. But just as Lawrence had been the master mind in the desert war, now he was the guiding spirit and adviser who showed the Arab delegates what diplomatic moves to make. When the peace conference was over the claims of the Arabs were only partly satisfied. Syria was split up in a ridiculous manner, part of it going to the French and part to the Arabs. Still, Emir Feisal got Damascus, the ancient capital of the old Arabian Empire, and became its king. A few months later, however, the French forced Feisal and his followers to flee. Lawrence felt the bitter injustice of it. Feisal and his Arab followers were losing nearly all that they had been promised in return for helping the Allies smash the Turks and Germans. The promises that had been made were not kept. Disappointed with the Allied ingratitude, and naturally shy anyhow, the boyish Oxford student, who had commanded an Oriental army, tried to hide himself away in England. He refused all the high honors and military decorations that were offered to him. The Arabs wanted to make him an important man in their country and tried to shower gifts on him. But he decided to stay away from Arabia. He knew that, while the Bedouins would follow him as long as a war was on, and as long as he was leading them on spectacular raids and blowing up bridges and trains, they would never allow a foreigner to rule them in time of peace. So instead of being a help to his friend Emir Feisal and the other Arab leaders, Lawrence felt that in the end he would be a hindrance.

The heads of the British government wanted to give him high position. They wanted to award him the Victoria Cross, the highest honor that any man in the British Empire can get for heroism. They wanted to make him a knight. But he refused everything. He did not want power. He hated the lime-light. He cared nothing for knighthood. And as for money, he did not know what to do with it. He is one of those fellows for whom money has scarcely any value. He would rather work for the fun of working, lead armies and do great deeds for the personal satisfaction, rather than for any reward. After the peace conference he told his friends that he preferred to go off to some quiet corner and spend a year or two reading the books that he loved so much.

Sometime later I delivered a lecture in

London on Lawrence and his exploits and showed the motion-pictures we had taken of his Bedouins in the desert. Naturally I wanted to look him up, and let him see how his old companions looked on the screen. But no one knew where he was. He seemed to have vanished. Then I received a note:

My dear Lowell Thomas:

I saw your show last night. And thank God the lights were out!

T. E. LAWRENCE.

Thank God the lights were out! He was as much afraid of being recognized as that. Later on he had tea one afternoon with my wife and me. He begged me to stop telling about his exploits in public. He had been living in a little furnished room without being known, having been driven into seclusion by autograph fiends, reporters, editors, publishers, and representatives of the gentler sex. He said that my first two weeks of lectures about him at the Royal Opera House in London had resulted in his getting twenty-eight proposals of marriage from unknown ladies and that they were continuing to arrive by every mail, most of them by way of Oxford.

After this, finding his hiding-place discovered, he retired to Oxford, to the cloisters of All Souls College, where he had been elected a research fellow. His fellowship gave him an income and a place to study. Even there he lived mostly by night and slept during the day, to escape admirers who tried to intrude on him. During this time he continued writing an account of his adventures in Arabia, a marvelous scholarly work. He had almost finished it when one day, on his way from London to Oxford, with the manuscript in a black bag, it was stolen from him, and the two hundred thousand words he had written were gone. He never got the manuscript back and eventually wrote his book all over again.

In 1921 the British government induced him to take a post in the Colonial Office as adviser on Arab affairs. Lawrence accepted for a period of one year. He attended to his duties faithfully, and it was largely due to his influence in the Colonial Office that his old friend, Emir Feisal, was made king of Iraq. The very day his twelve months expired, Lawrence put on his hat, walked out of his office in Whitehall, and vanished as mysteriously as he and his raggle-taggle Bedouins used to do when he was raiding Turkish troop trains during the World War.

Where he was remained a mystery for some time, until the news leaked out that Colonel Lawrence was in the British army, a private, a mere Tommy, in the air force. One day an officer looked hard at a soldier. Private Ross was this soldier's name, but the officer could not mistake that blond boyish face.

"Lawrence of Arabia," he said to himself.

The enterprising officer sold to a newspaper the astonishing information that the uncrowned king of the desert, the youth who had made two kings and a sultan, was a Tommy in the air force. The news made a sensation, and "Private Ross" was made the object of much curiosity and attention. A few days later he disappeared.

Sometime later a recruit joined a company in the tank corps. The other Tommies noticed that he was a curious chap, shy, retiring, silent, and rather well educated. He was polite and friendly and unassuming, but he did not mix in very well and kept to himself. He was known as Private Shaw. One day they saw in a newspaper a picture of Lawrence of Arabia. It looked very much like Private Shaw. But, no, it couldn't be. Imagine Private Shaw a colonel and the mysterious hero Lawrence. It was absurd, and yet it was so. Another Tommy saw an envelop sticking from beneath the pillow of Private Shaw's bunk. He took a look at it. It was addressed to Colonel Thomas E. Lawrence.

How Lawrence came to take the name of Shaw is an amusing story. George Bernard

Shaw and he have long been friends. One day the uncrowned king of Arabia dropped in for tea at the house of the famous dramatist. One of the ladies present glanced at him admiringly. He looked very young, with his light hair, delicate complexion, and small slender frame. He might have been a boy from preparatory school. The lady turned to Mrs. Shaw.

"What an intelligent looking son you have!" she exclaimed.

Lawrence howled with delight when he heard this, and swore that he would thereafter be known as Shaw, since he had been inadvertently adopted into the dramatist's family. The result was that when he soon afterward hid himself in the tank corps he enlisted as Private Shaw.

One summer, while I was staying on the south coast of England, I received a welcome visit from Lawrence's old tent-mate, Major William E. Marshall, the distinguished Scottish scientist who was known in Arabia as the "fighting bacteriologist," and who after the war was British adviser to the king of Hedjaz. Major Marshall told me that he had called on Lawrence not long before and had seen on his desk a copy of Shaw's "Saint Joan." He picked it up and discovered on the fly-leaf the inscription: "From Public Shaw to Private Shaw."

After Private Shaw was found out in the tanks corps he vanished again, and nothing much was heard about him until the recent publication of his remarkable book, "Revolt in the Desert." Some say that he is now in India with the Royal Air Force, others that he has returned to Arabia to pursue his archæological work. He has always been an archæologist at heart, and when he told me the story of how he had beaten the Turks at Petra, the rose-red city half as old as time, he said he regarded the fighting and the victory as small matters. What really counted was the beauty and significance of the ruins of the one-time great and populous city.

In all now I have told the story of Lawrence's adventures, and shown our motion record of his desert campaign, to some four thousand audiences, and in every part of the world where I have lectured people have asked me the same question:

"What was the secret of this amazing young man's success?"

Millions of people have wondered how a Christian and a European could gain such influence over fanatical Mohammedans. Nor is the question difficult to answer. Among the reasons why he won the admiration of the picturesque warriors of Arabia are the following: They admired him because he could outdo them at the very things which they do better than any one else, such as camel riding and shooting. They admired him because of his daring and his reckless courage, and because he never boasted of his deeds. In fact he usually gave all the credit to his companions. The Arabs loved that. So do all of us. They followed him because when he led them in battle and was wounded in action he kept right on fighting. Six times during the campaign was Lawrence wounded, but fortunately none of the wounds were fatal and all healed without medical attention. So the Arabs thought that Lawrence bore a charmed life, and that he surely must have been sent down from heaven by their Prophet Mohammed to free them from the Turks. They admired him intensely because he was always either victorious or followed up a defeat by a victory.

But there were many other reasons why he succeeded in doing what no other European had ever accomplished and what no Oriental had been able to do for nearly a thousand years. They admired young Lawrence because of his keen and sparkling wit and were amazed to find that, although a mere youth, he seemed endowed with the wisdom of their wise men. Then too he was a brilliant leader and military strategist. He could match wits with the keenest Oriental diplomats, and his uncanny knowledge of classic Arabic, combined with his ability to speak nearly all their widely different dialects, dumfounded them. How could a stranger speak their tongue with greater facility than they themselves?

Had Lawrence worn European clothes and held to his European habits he never could have succeeded in the unparalleled way that he did. When he went into the desert he took off his Western garments, threw aside his Western ways, and became a Bedouin. For centuries to come the name of "Sidi Laurens," as they called him, will be a legend. Around the desert camp-fires in the years that are to come the stories of his deeds will be told by eagle-eyed, hawk-nosed sons of Ishmael, just as to-day the sheiks of Araby sing of the deeds of Omar, Abu Bekr, Ali, and the mighty warrior Khalid.

During his many years of wandering up and down the desert, dressing like an Arab, living with Arabs in their tents, observing their customs, talking to them in their own dialects, riding on his camel across the sand-dunes, and lying down at night under a silent dome of stars, back in those days before the Great War found him, Ned Lawrence drank the cup of Arabian wisdom and absorbed the spirit of the nomad peoples. Then when the World War brought him his opportunity this youth united the scattered tribes of Arabia and induced chieftains who had been bitter enemies for ages to forget their blood-feuds and fight side by side for the same cause. From remote parts of the desert the swarthy tribesmen swarmed to his standard as if he had been a new prophet. By his genius, his wisdom, and his courage, this Oxford youth brought victory to the Arabs. What will become of him? No man can foretell, and I doubt if Lawrence himself cares. Glory, fame, personal popularity, and the lime-light mean nothing to him. Unless some new crisis should bring him to the front again we may hear little more of him.

When an undergraduate at Oxford, he

and another student made a solemn compact that if either ever did anything particularly noteworthy he would telegraph for the other to come so that they could celebrate the event. In 1920, after his return from the war and from the peace conference, after he had made two kings and a sultan, and after he had led a great army and played an important part in freeing Arabia, Palestine, Syria, and Mesopotamia from the Turks, Ned Lawrence telegraphed his college chum as follows:

Come at once. Have done something.

This was the first word that had passed between the two since their college days ten years before. When his chum arrived, this is what Ned Lawrence had done that he thought worth celebrating: He had just finished building a little bungalow for himself on the edge of Epping Forest, and was keeping cows!

One thing is certain: Ned Lawrence will not permit his country to make a hero out of him. But historians of the future will probably rank him among the most remarkable men that ever lived, men like Leif the Lucky, Sir Francis Drake, Clive of India, Marco Polo, and "Chinese" Gordon of Khartum.